JavaScript Object Programming

Martin Rinehart

Apress®

JavaScript Object Programming

ISBN-13 (pbk): 978-1-4842-1786-3

ISBN-13 (electronic): 978-1-4842-1787-0

Managing Director: Welmoed Spahr
Lead Editor: Jeffrey Pepper
Editorial Board: Steve Anglin, Pramila Balan, Louise Corrigan, Jonathan Gennick,
    Robert Hutchinson, Celestin Suresh John, Michelle Lowman, James Markham,
    Susan McDermott, Matthew Moodie, Jeffrey Pepper, Douglas Pundick,
    Ben Renow-Clarke, Gwenan Spearing
Coordinating Editor: Mark Powers
Copy Editor: Kezia Endsley
Compositor: SPi Global
Indexer: SPi Global
Artist: SPi Global

Distributed to the book trade worldwide by Springer Science+Business Media New York, 233 Spring Street, 6th Floor, New York, NY 10013. Phone 1-800-SPRINGER, fax (201) 348-4505, e-mail orders-ny@springer-sbm.com, or visit www.springeronline.com. Apress Media, LLC is a California LLC and the sole member (owner) is Springer Science + Business Media Finance Inc (SSBM Finance Inc). SSBM Finance Inc is a Delaware corporation.

For information on translations, please e-mail rights@apress.com, or visit www.apress.com.

Apress and friends of ED books may be purchased in bulk for academic, corporate, or promotional use. eBook versions and licenses are also available for most titles. For more information, reference our Special Bulk Sales–eBook Licensing web page at www.apress.com/bulk-sales.

Any source code or other supplementary materials referenced by the author in this text is available to readers at www.apress.com/9781484217863. For detailed information about how to locate your book's source code, go to www.apress.com/source-code/. Readers can also access source code at SpringerLink in the Supplementary Material section for each chapter.

Dedicated to Brendan Eich. He wrote JavaScript in 1995 giving us its object literals and object programming.

JSW: JSWindows, v2

Vox clamantis lorem ipsum

Window_M Rules! X

Window_M #2 X

Contents at a Glance

Contents

About the Author

Martin Rinehart, a self-confessed JavaScript lover, set aside work on his five-volume frontend-engineering textbook project for long enough to write this small book on JavaScript inheritance. He wanted to eliminate some of the massive confusion surrounding this important subject. (Veterans of classical OOP backgrounds, and Martin is one, have to unlearn much of what they think they "know." Veteran JavaScripters have to stop abusing the prototype chain.) Martin is the author of over a dozen books on programming, and of the JSWindows system that brings a windowing UI to browser-based applications.

A Note for the Implementers

JavaScript, or more exactly, the subset of JavaScript Crockford identifies as "The Good Parts," is a beautiful language. It is small, yet expressive. Its functional programming and object programming gives it extraordinary depth. In nearly a half century of programming I have used dozens of languages. Only two of them, JavaScript being one, have been languages I've loved.

Today there are people working to free JavaScript from the browser, to further empower JavaScript (WebGL, to mention a personal favorite) and to bring it up to professional speed. My apologies to the latter group. In many ways, object programming is the enemy of compiled speed.

So a word of encouragement and advice to our courageous implementers. First, making JavaScript run at some reasonable fraction of C's speed is a magnificent goal. More power to you! (And yes, that's self-serving. You are giving more power to all of us who write JavaScript. We love it and we thank you for it.)

Second, removing object programming to gain speed cuts out the heart to save the patient. Object programming is not your enemy, it is the essence of the language. Look on it as a challenge, as the Everest of your profession. The view from the top will be spectacular. Object programming at half the speed of C will be breathtaking.

—Martin Rinehart, 15 November, 2015
Delaware Valley, Pennsylvania, USA

Introduction

Hanover, NH. September, 1965. Dartmouth's incoming freshmen were told to go to an hour-long lecture by Professor John G. Kemeny. Being incoming freshmen, we went. Along with Kurtz, Kemeny had designed a new computer language called BASIC. It was supposed to be much easier to learn than existing languages. In an hour Kemeny taught us how to use most of it. (And he made us laugh a lot, too. He was a great teacher.)

I was lucky to be there then. Kemeny told us to go write a program to compute the value of pi. Using Dartmouth's new, time-sharing computer system and a teletype terminal (which punched your program into paper tape in lieu of disk storage), I actually got pi to two decimal places. My career as a mathematician (the reason I had chosen Dartmouth) ended and my career as a programmer began. I've been coding ever since.

During the last half century I've watched software revolutions come and go. Mostly go. Only two have really stuck. First, structured programming let us get rid of goto statements in the late 70s. And then there was the object revolution that started in the 80s. Objects had completely taken over before the end of the century.

I remember when fourth and fifth generation languages were going to take over from C and BASIC. C and BASIC are still here.

Maybe some of you remember the component revolution that was going to replace object-oriented programming.

Threaded interpreters (remember Forth?) were going to take over the software world.

JavaScript, with its hybrid class-based/prototypal model, is leading the way in objects. I bet that others will be copying it. But I've learned that predicting the future is not a science. I've been right, sometimes. I was right when I decided to switch from C to C++. (There have been other times. Mercifully, I'm forgetting more these days.)

I left C for C++ in the early 90s. I left C++ (it was getting big and heavy) for Java in 95. When I first started using object-oriented programming in JavaScript (2006), I looked for all my old friends. Classes, for one. They weren't there. (More exactly, I didn't see them.) But the language was good, there were no thoughts I couldn't implement, and so in a week I'd tricked out JavaScript to behave like my old friends. And, in my ignorance, lost the best parts of JavaScript. By 2008, my JavaScript had started to look like JavaScript.

In 50 years I've used lots of languages. Two I've loved. JavaScript is one of them. Mostly it's the object programming that I love. (Well, that plus the functional programming, which I really mean to master one of these days.)

This book is about object programming. Hope you enjoy it.

CHAPTER 1

Creating Objects

Objects were a software experiment that worked. They were invented in the 1960s and in research labs in the 1970s. They became the new, mainstream programming paradigm in the 1980s. By the 90s, languages that were being created (Java, JavaScript, Python, and Ruby) were all object-oriented. Languages that predated objects were being retrofitted. Today, even the latest versions of 50-year-old languages (BASIC, Cobol, and Fortran) have adopted objects.

In this book, we will be examining two object models supported by JavaScript. We need to understand the benefits of objects to see how these alternatives provide the benefits of programming with objects (or not).

Reasons for Objects

There are a lot of reasons to prefer programming with objects. We'll discuss three here.

Objects Do Methods

First, the syntax has "things doing things" just as happens outside of the world of software. The things that objects do are small software programs. They are functions that the object can perform, commonly called methods. If you program a dog (object) to speak (method), you express it directly:

```
dog.speak(); // "Woof, woof"
```

Many objects can implement the same action (method) with variations appropriate for each, as Listing 1-1 shows.

Listing 1-1

```
parrot.speak(); // "Polly want a cracker."
kitten.speak(); // "mew, mew"
```

If your parrots and kittens use different methods for speaking, object systems will choose the appropriate method for you. Chapter 8 explains *subtype polymorphism*, the principle underlying the selection of object-appropriate methods.

Event-Driven Programming

Second, few programs now do anything except by user direction. Most programs paint an interface (menus, icons, and buttons) and wait for a user command. This is called "event-driven" programming. When the user clicks the Save icon, the user's document is written to disk. Internally, the user action could trigger a very small program:

```
user_data.save();
```

Again, it uses the `noun.verb()` syntax. This brings us to the main reason for the success of objects.

Taming Exponential Complexity

As programs grow in size, complexity increases exponentially. We have all used systems that never seemed to be robust. Fixing this broke that. If the complexity is ever successfully tamed, it is after immense expense. Objects help shrink the size and limit the complexity. That reduces the effort (expense).

Let's think about a simple example. A small non-object program might require a thousand lines of code. The same job using objects might require ten methods, each only a hundred lines of code. The ten small methods will be far cheaper to write and vastly cheaper to debug.

As we look at JSWindows' code, you will see many features that take surprisingly little code and live comfortably outside of other parts of the system.

Class-Based vs. Prototypal

Objects come in many guises. We will be using class-based object-oriented programming (OOP, based on classes) and JavaScript's hybrid class/prototypal object model. To understand these we look back at JavaScript's predecessors.

Simula

Objects and classes ("classes" meaning the software that creates objects) were built into the Simula 67 version of the Simula language by its Norwegian creators, Dahl and Nygaard. They called their new paradigm "object-oriented."

Simula, a language for modeling simulations, was ahead of its time but would prove immensely influential in the history of computer programming.

Smalltalk

Simula was studied by Alan Kay *et. al.* at Xerox Palo Alto Research Center (Xerox PARC). They designed and coded Smalltalk, first released to the public as Smalltalk-80 (1980). According to Kay, Smalltalk featured pure object-oriented programming (OOP). Objects were created from classes and classes were objects.

Smalltalk was widely publicized and people began to discuss this new paradigm as a possible future direction for programming. *Byte* magazine devoted its August, 1980 issue to Smalltalk-80. Even my tiny consulting company had a programmer working in Smalltalk. (Programming productivity and our bottom line were very tightly coupled.)

C++ and Java

Simula was used by graduate student Bjarne Stroustrup (a Dane studying at Cambridge, simulating multi-computer systems). He wrote, "... ever since [using Simula] I have seen classes as the proper primary focus of program design." Simula, however, was too slow for Stroustrup's purposes.

At Bell Labs, Doctor Stroustrup designed and coded "C with classes." His compiler was released (1983) as "C++." His OOP language ran at the speed of C programs but was less object-oriented than Smalltalk. Classes in C++, for example, were not objects.

Despite criticism from the Smalltalk community (classes should be objects!), C++ style OOP is the largest branch of modern OOP.

The C++ OOP model has been widely copied by languages such as Java (1995). There are differences in details (C++ supported multiple inheritance; instead Java used interfaces), but the heart is the same: a class provides object instance definitions, object method code, and a constructor for creating objects during execution. Objects have the properties specified by the definition. Their data properties' values can be modified during execution.

Many other languages—such as C#, Visual Basic, Cobol, and Fortran—have copied the basic C++ model. OOP has become, for many, synonymous with Stroustrup's class-based object model and this book will use the term that way. Today, the C++ family OOP languages dominate all programming outside browsers.

Self and JavaScript

While C++ conquered the programming world with its not-quite-pure object orientation, work continued at Xerox PARC. Smith and Ungar created the Self system. Self (1986) contradicted both Kay and Stroustrup by creating objects using other objects as prototypes. It has no classes. It featured an early object literal notation and dynamic object programming in which object properties could be added and deleted during program execution.

The Self team moved from PARC to Stanford and then to Sun Microsystems. Research on Self had nearly ended by April, 1995, when another company in Silicon Valley, Netscape, hired Brendan Eich, an experienced implementer of computer languages. Netscape wanted him to create a scripting language for its Navigator browser.

Eich based his new language's object model on Self's prototypal approach and supported C++-like object creation syntax. The language was named JavaScript (although its only relationship to Sun's Java was in the marketing). It was released later in 1995. Today JavaScript is highly successful as the only language available for programming inside all major browsers and it is a leading choice for programming the client end of all mobile applications. It is also used for some server-side programming.

At first, JavaScript was used for making minor tweaks, often purely cosmetic, to web pages. In the first decade of the 21st Century, two things promoted JavaScript into mainstream programming prominence. A new technology bundle named "Ajax" enhanced browser/server communication enabling applications such as Google's Gmail. (Gmail's public testing began in 2004.) And Douglas Crockford, a senior JavaScript guru wrote a book, *JavaScript, The Good Parts* (2008), which identified and praised the language's core capabilities.

JavaScript's prototypal/OOP hybrid object model is now a second major object-oriented approach.

So what are objects?

Objects Up Close

An *object* is a collection of properties (often a set, but "set" has a mathematical meaning we do not want here). Properties are named values. Values may be, depending on the language, simple values (Boolean, integer, or character), composite values built from other values (arrays or objects) or, in languages capable of functional programming, functions or other blocks of code. (JavaScript also implements functional programming borrowed from the Scheme language, a dialect of Lisp.)

In JavaScript, property names must be strings. In most class-based OOP languages they must be strings that are limited by the restrictions imposed on variable names.

Some authors use the word "property" to specifically mean what we call "data properties"—properties that are not methods.

Data Properties

Objects may have data properties. These are often said to describe an object's "state." A dog might have properties such as name, breed, and date-of-birth. Each dog (called an "object instance" or, in class-based OOP, an "instance" of the dog class) will have space allocated to store each of these properties' values. The key point is that each instance has its own set of data properties.

Methods (Code Properties)

Objects also are permitted direct access to a collection of functions (commonly called "instance methods") that are part of the class software (in class-based languages) or the prototype (in JavaScript). These functions are separate from, but available to, the objects.

All dogs, in the example above, could access the speak() method:

```
dog.speak(); // says "Woof, woof"
```

Here, speak() is a property of dog objects. In the text, trailing parentheses indicate that the property is executable code. This is one of the two main categories of object properties. Unlike data, the methods are stored in the class software, in class-based OOP, or in the prototype, in JavaScript. (As methods require storage space, it would be extremely inefficient to store a separate copy of each method with each instance of the class.)

Methods operate on the data properties of each instance. If each dog had a "message" property, a small breed could say, "Yap, yap" while a large breed said "Woof, woof." If an application's dogs could speak a bit of English, the programmer might combine fixed values with the dog's name property to achieve a result like Listing 1-2.

Listing 1-2

```
collie.speak(); // "My name is Lassie."

beagle.speak(); // "My name is Snoopy."
```

Now that you know where we've been and where we are, you can think about the three ways of creating JavaScript objects:

- From nothing (*ex nihilo*, often using object notation)
- From OOP class-like functions
- From prototype objects

Ex Nihilo Object Creation

In Self, most objects are created by cloning a similar object. Which raised this issue: where do you get the first object? Self solved this problem by allowing the creation of objects *ex nihilo* (from nothing). Eich adopted this Self idea for JavaScript.

There are two direct ways to create a JavaScript object from nothing. You can use the Object constructor or an object literal.

The Object Constructor

In JavaScript there is an object constructor, Object(). All objects you create will be created, directly or indirectly, from Object(). You can use it explicitly with OOP-standard syntax:

```
my_object = new Object();
```

As the name suggests, this creates an object. The initial capital letter tells you, in a JavaScript program, that the Object() function was intended for use after the new operator as a constructor. When you create an object this way you can assign properties, as Listing 1-3 shows.

Listing 1-3

```
my_object.size = 'large';
my_object.color = 'blue';
```

If you come to JavaScript from an OOP background, as I did, this is somewhat strange. Where did these properties come from? The object.property syntax, on the left side of an assignment, will assign a value to an existing property or, if the specified property name is not found, it will create and then assign to a new property. Sounds like chaos if you're used to class-based object definitions. A simple typo means you've created a new property when you meant to assign to an existing one. Turns out that this is not a problem in practice. (You can turn this off, if it scares you. See Appendices G and H. But please don't. Write JavaScript as it was intended. See Appendix I if you want to laugh at one programmer who was slow to take JavaScript as it was designed.)

Properties may be added to objects any time that you choose. (Rubyists call this "meta programming." Pythonistas speak of "dynamic properties." Early JavaScripters spoke of "expando properties." More on this in Chapter 2.) Note that this is a key difference from the standard Stroustrup OOP model where a set of properties is defined by the class and cannot be changed during execution.

Object Literals

Eich invented a very simple but powerful object literal notation using the classless Self ideas. Listing 1-4 shows an object literal creating an *ex nihilo* object.

Listing 1-4

```
my_object = {
    size: 'large',
    color: 'blue'
};
```

Property names (size and color in this example) are strings but, as Listing 1-2 shows, you may omit the quotes (unless you insist on space characters in your property names). As in C, use of whitespace is for readability. The following line does the same job.

```
my_object={size:'large',color:'blue'};
```

You may think of the basic Object instance (foo = new Object();) as an empty object (with no properties). That's a mental model, not literal truth. Appendixes G and H tell you more about the internals of an "empty" object. Note: foo = {}; is the easy way to get an "empty" object.

The object literal notation (documented by Crockford as JSON, JavaScript Object Notation) is still a common method for creating objects from nothing. However, the Object() constructor was assigned powerful new capabilities in the ECMAScript 2015 standard and some top JavaScript programmers always call it explicitly to create their objects. (See Appendixes G and H.) I prefer the object literal's readability.

Object.prototype (we'll discuss this in depth when we get to prototypal object creation) gives all objects some properties. For example, you get a toString() method that reports "[object Object]," telling you that the type is "object" and its constructor is Object(). (Having your console tell you than an object is an object is almost useless.)

Creating your own objects lets you supply useful toString() methods. If you alert() or console.log() an object you will be looking at its toString() value (except in Chrome). Assuming that my_object is an important object in the code you are debugging, you will want to give it a toString() method showing its important properties. Listing 1-5 shows one alternative.

Listing 1-5

```
my_object = {
    size: 'large',
    color: 'blue'
    toString: function() { return
        'size:' + this.size +
        ', color:' + this.color; }
};
```

To get a toString() report from every browser, force coercion of your object to a string before you look at it. It's easy:

```
console.log('' + object);.
```

You will use *ex nihilo* objects whenever you want a single, unique object. You will use OOP-style or prototypal creation when you want multiple objects that are similar or identical. (Compare the simplicity of the JavaScript *ex nihilo* object to the equivalent OOP object following the singleton pattern.)

Bear in mind that when you write:

```
my_object = { ... properties here ...);
```

The variable my_object is not an object. It is a reference to an object. The actual object is somewhere in memory. A reference is a memory address or an index into a table or part of some other mechanism the implementers choose to find the object when needed. This will vary from one JavaScript to another. If you write foo = my_object; you create a second reference to the object, not a second object.

More *Ex Nihilo* Objects

Arrays and functions are also objects in JavaScript. Here an array literal creates an array.

```
arr = ['dog', 'cat', 'mouse'];
```

This standard syntax creates a function:

```
function foo(args) { ... foo code ... }
```

You can also create an anonymous function with a variable as a reference:

```
var bar = function(args) { ... bar code ... }
```

7

These also create objects from nothing. From now on, however, this book will reserve the adjective *ex nihilo* for objects that are neither functions nor arrays.

You might ask yourself if creating objects "from nothing" follows the standard OOP model or the prototypal model. We'll ask again in Chapter 6 when we create an *ex nihilo* class.

OOP-Style Object Creation

You can use OOP-style code when you want to create multiple similar objects that use a common set of methods but vary by their data values. For this you write your own constructors, just as you do in class-based languages.

There is a major difference at the design stage, however. In OOP you design with great care. The properties you did not see at the outset may disrupt a considerable effort. In OOP all the objects of one class are identical. In JavaScript, all the objects of a class should be similar, but need not be identical. Your tolerance for design errors is much higher.

Constructors

By convention, the name of a JavaScript constructor begins with a capital letter. The constructor function creates properties, commonly data properties, and adds initial values. Listing 1-6 shows a simple example.

Listing 1-6

```
function Dog(name, breed) {
    var new_dog = this; // the 'new' object

    new_dog.name = name;
    new_dog.breed = breed;
}
```

The pattern in Listing 1-6, where the value of the parameter name becomes the value of the name property, is very common.

Assigning Initial Property Values

Using the Dog() constructor, your Dog() objects can start their lives with two properties, name and breed. Listing 1-7 shows this constructor being used to create Dog() objects.

Listing 1-7

```
var snoopy = new Dog('Snoopy', 'Beagle');
var lassie = new Dog('Lassie', 'Collie');
```

Familiar object.property notation can be used to access these properties' values.

```
alert(snoopy.breed); // Beagle
```

Creating Instance Methods

Listing 1-8 shows an instance method placed in the prototype property of the constructor.

Listing 1-8

```
Dog.prototype.speak = function() {
    return "Woof! Woof!";
}

snoopy.speak(); // Woof! Woof!
lassie.speak(); // Woof! Woof!
```

We'll examine the prototype in detail later in this chapter. For now, the value of a property not in the instance (the speak() method in this example) will be the value of that property in the prototype.

A reference to the object(snoopy in snoopy.speak() is passed to instance method (speak() in snoopy.speak()) as the this variable. If you want a dog to identify itself, use the function in Listing 1-9.

Listing 1-9

```
Dog.prototype.who_am_i = function() {
    return "I'm " + this.name;
}

lassie.who_am_i(); // I'm Lassie
```

Creating Class Statics

Class-wide data (data that applies to every instance) can be attached as a property of the constructor, as Listing 1-10 shows.

Listing 1-10

```
Dog.diet = "carnivore"; // not prototype
alert(lassie.diet); // undefined

Dog.prototype.diet = "carnivore";
alert(lassie.diet); // carnivore
```

Getters and Setters

All JavaScript property values are public. You can create genuine private values with closures (see Appendix F). The following example adopts the JavaScript convention that properties beginning with an underscore character should not be accessed directly.

Listing 1-11

```
lassie._private = "Verified data.";
Dog.prototype.get_private =
    function () { return this._private; }

lassie.get_private(); // Verified data.
```

Default Values

Assume that the Dog constructor call may or may not include the breed value. Listing 1-12 shows one way to access a default value.

Listing 1-12

```
function Dog(name, breed) {
    this.name = name;
    if (breed) { this.breed = breed; }
}
Dog.prototype.breed = 'mixed breed';

var mutt = new Dog( 'Mutt' );
mutt.breed // mixed breed
```

At this point, you should see that the class constructor, including its prototype property, is very similar to the classes in Stroustrup's OOP. The mechanism is different but the result is the same. Next we look at creating objects from prototypes, which is a different technique altogether. (Prototypes are used in both OOP-style and prototypal object creation, but the results are not the same.)

Prototypal Object Creation

In Self, objects are created by cloning other objects. You can use this technique in JavaScript, too. (You do not have to choose either OOP-style or prototypal style for a JavaScript system. You should choose based on the reality each family of objects is modeling.)

Let's begin by looking more closely at object prototypes.

Object Prototypes

When JavaScript sees an object property name, such as "color" in object.color, it looks to the object for a property of that name. If the name does not exist it looks to the object's prototype for a property of that name. (The prototype is another object.)

Assume that you created singers, as Listing 1-13 shows.

Listing 1-13

```
function Singer() {}; // no properties
var patty   = new Singer(),
    maxene  = new Singer(),
    laverne = new Singer();

patty.sing(); // error, undefined method
```

There is no sing() method, so these girls don't know how to sing. In Listing 1-14 we teach Patty, individually.

Listing 1-14

```
patty.sing = function () {
    return '...boogie woogie bugle boy...';
}
patty.sing(); //...boogie woogie bugle boy...
```

Patty can sing, but her sisters cannot. You could have put a sing() method in the prototype, as in Listing 1-15.

Listing 1-15

```
Singer.prototype.sing = function () {
    return '...blows eight-to-the-bar...';
};
patty.sing(); // boogie woogie bugle boy
maxene.sing(); // blows eight-to-the-bar
laverne.sing(); // blows eight-to-the-bar
```

How do you know that Singer.prototype was the prototype for our singing sisters? If Singer() is the constructor, then Singer.prototype is the prototype. The prototype for any object you create from a constructor is the property named "prototype" of the constructor function from which the object was instantiated. (Chapter 9 fills in all the details of the underlying mechanism by which Singer.prototype becomes the prototype for all Singer() family instances. Mastering these details will make you shine on interviews. It will make very little difference to the code you write.)

In the class-based model, instance methods are written in the class software. In Java you would have created a sing() method in Singer.java. In JavaScript you assign the sing() method to the Singer() function's prototype property. The result is the same. The objects created from the constructor can sing().

(The Andrews Sisters—Patty, Maxene, and LaVerne—had their biggest hit, of many, with "Boogie Woogie Bugle Boy" in 1941. The video has not stood the test of time but the music is still great. http://www.dump.com/andrewssisters/, 2:21)

The Prototype Chain

Now let's repeat the paragraph that started the previous section:

> When JavaScript sees an object property name, such as
> "color," in object.color it looks to the object for a property
> of that name. If the name does not exist it looks to the object's
> prototype for a property of that name. (The prototype is
> another object.)

What happens if JavaScript does not find the name in the prototype? "The prototype is another object." Simply read the paragraph again. JavaScript will look in the prototype's prototype. In JavaScript, all objects you create are either created from the Object constructor, and therefore Object.prototype is their prototype, or their constructor's prototype is an object created from Object, or their constructor's constructor is an object created from Object, and so on.

Searching prototypes stops at Object.prototype. This is called the prototype chain. Ultimately, Object.prototype is the prototype of every object you create, directly or indirectly.

Bear in mind the following two facts as you consider the prototype chain.

First, there are large families of objects (not ones that you create) that may not have prototypes. JavaScript does not know how to do input or output. It depends on a "host environment" for all I/O. Most commonly, JavaScript runs in a browser that provides the host environment through objects. These are called "host objects" and unless the browser's authors were meticulous (most weren't) the host objects do not have prototypes.

Second, you can see how the prototype chain could be used to implement class-based inheritance. Presume Collie extends Dog in an OOP inheritance chain. If you could connect your Collie family objects so that properties not found in Collie.prototype would be sought in Dog.prototype, you would have OOP-style inheritance. What does not follow is that this would be a good way to achieve OOP-style inheritance. There are other ways that are often preferable.

Object Prototype Cloning

For prototypal creation you start with an object. We'll start with an *ex nihilo* Lassie in Listing 1-16.

Listing 1-16

```
var lassie = {
    name: 'Lassie',
    breed: 'Collie',
    speak: function () {
        return 'Woof! Woof!'; }
};
```

Next, you can make a clone of Lassie with the `create()` method of the `Object()` constructor:

```
var snoopy = Object.create(lassie);
```

Snoopy is now a reference to an empty (no properties) object. Snoopy's prototype is the `Lassie` object. If you ask him to talk he'll tell you:

```
snoopy.speak(); // Woof! Woof!
```

This is just what you want. Unfortunately if you ask Snoopy for his name and breed, he thinks he's a Collie named Lassie. By using `Lassie` for a prototype, all her clones will share her instance data properties. This is seldom what you want.

To understand the next example we'll introduce object subscript notation and the `for/in` loop. In OOP you write `snoopy.name`. That's fine in JavaScript, too. For programming with object properties JavaScript allows `snoopy['name']`, too. That's a nuisance to type if you want a particular property, but it is invaluable if you want to do something with all the properties of an object. It lets you use variables. If you loop through all of the properties of snoopy (`for (prop in snoopy)` does that job), `snoopy[prop]` will address the properties one at a time.

You could have written a little clone method, like the one in Listing 1-17.

Listing 1-17

```
var clone = function(proto_obj) {
    var ret = {}; // 'empty' object

    for ( var prop in proto_obj ) {
        ret[prop] = proto_obj[prop]; }

    return ret;
}
```

You could use this function, `snoopy = clone(lassie)`, to create a new object with a copy of each of `lassie`'s properties. With this brute-force clone, `lassie`'s properties are also snoopy's properties. (Note: You could not just say `snoopy = lassie; `. That would create a second reference to the same object. Any change to snoopy would also change lassie, and vice versa.)

You probably wanted Lassie's data properties to become Snoopy's data properties while Lassie's method properties become Snoopy's prototype's properties. After Chapter 2, you'll know more than enough to write a function that automates this for you. I don't recommend that you do so, however. In all cases you'll still have the problem that Snoopy's name property will have the string `'Lassie'` as its value, for one example. This will be easy enough to fix if you are only making one or two clones, but the classic OOP pattern is generally easier if you want lots of similar objects that differ in their data properties' values.

At present there is an argument within the JavaScript community about the use of OOP-style object creation. Some say you should avoid it entirely. I think this is wrong.

JavaScript supports prototypal and OOP-style object creation. The latter is particularly convenient when you want to create lots of objects in a family that differs in the values of its objects' data properties. There are millions of OOP programmers and billions of lines of OOP code. Clearly, this is a common way of solving coding problems. When it works, use it. But when you use it, put common values (data and/or methods) into the prototype.

Summary

We use objects because the object.method() syntax is a good fit for a lot of real-world activity, because they fit well in event-driven programming and they help turn monolithic blocks of code into smaller, easier-to-debug pieces.

JavaScript supports two distinct models. The object/class combination dates back to the Simula language in 1967. By 1980 Smalltalk had evolved at Xerox PARC to a pure form in which classes created objects and classes were, themselves objects. Stroustrup's C++ created the first major branch of modern OOP in spite of being less than pure. (Its classes are not objects.) Self evolved from Smalltalk and eliminated classes altogether by prototypal object inheritance (objects clone other objects). JavaScript combines class-based and prototypal approaches.

JavaScript supports creation of *ex nihilo* objects (from nothing) as well as OOP-like and prototypal object creation.

Next, we go on to programming with objects, comparing JavaScript's nearly unlimited flexibility to the more common restrictions of class-based OOP.

CHAPTER 2

■ ■ ■

Object Programming

I wrote a system, called JSWindows, for this book's predecessor. We'll describe it here and refer to it regularly for examples.

JSWindows Sample System

JSWindows is a basic windowing system (open/close windows, minimize/maximize, style, drag, and so on) written in JavaScript. It uses a heavy dose of OOP-style inheritance and lots of prototypal inheritance, too. You can try it yourself at my web site. You get the full source when you download this book's software:

Apress.com/9781484217863

Now, on to object programming.

OP Removes Restrictions

Once you can create objects, you are ready to consider object programming (OP) and some fundamental differences between JavaScript and OOP languages.

In class-based object-oriented programming the objects are defined before they are created. Once an object exists, you can execute its methods or assign values to its data properties. But you cannot add or delete properties or change methods, for example. What you can do with objects is limited by design. In JavaScript's object programming you can manipulate your objects in nearly unlimited ways. This is also by design.

OP Defined

The OOP model combines object instances, sets of name/value pairs, with class software. The class software provides a routine (the "constructor") to create instances, a place to store instance methods, and it provides other services. This is a subset of object programming. Let's define object programming as broadly as possible, eliminating classic OOP's restrictions:

- Objects are collections of properties. Properties are name/value pairs.

- An object programming (OP) system allows the creation, modification, and disposal of objects before and during program execution.

- "Modification" of objects means the ability to create, modify, and delete properties. Modifying properties includes modifying names and/or values. (Standard OOP allows modification of data property values.)

- An OP system also provides for services provided by OOP classes, such as storing data and code used by a family of objects (to avoid duplicating either in each instance [family member] object).

In practice, current objects are name/value pairs. (The ECMAScript standard says "key/value" but the keys must be strings.) In OOP, the names are restricted to the values legal for variable names. JavaScript names are any string values (including numbers, which are coerced to strings). I've never seen any practical advantage gained by JavaScript's greater freedom in property names as compared to standard OOP, but I have been disappointed occasionally by JavaScript's inability to use objects as keys.

Note that by this definition, the JavaScript OP model is incomplete as it does not allow direct modification of property keys. (It takes a three-line utility function to modify a property name. A direct approach would be preferable, but you can live without it.)

Programming with Properties

JavaScript leads programmers into object programming, almost without their being aware of it. Its two ways of identifying object properties play a major role.

Dot Notation

In the familiar `object.property` notation, a period separates the object reference from the property name. The latter is a constant in source code.

```
var x = object.prop_name;
```

In the above, `object` is the name of an object reference. `prop_name` is the name of a property of that object (directly, or via its prototype or prototype chain).

This is the common OOP notation, as well. Few OOP languages have the equivalent of JavaScript's subscript notation.

Subscript Notation

Subscript notation allows the use of variable property names. First, with a constant, the previous example is repeated here.

```
var x = object['prop_name'];
```

Listing 2-1 shows an example of an expression used to select a property.

Listing 2-1

```
var name = func_returning_prop_name(...);
var x = object[name];
```

Listing 2-2 shows both notations being used to create a new property within an object. Constant and variable property names are shown.

Listing 2-2

```
Object.new_prop = value;
Object['new_prop'] = value;

var name = func_returning_prop_name(...);
object[name] = value;
```

The combination of dot and subscript notations provides surprising power and grace when programming.

Object Programming Examples

In common JavaScript you will constantly add objects (combine two objects into one). Let's start OP with a utility to add objects.

Object Sum

JSWindows uses "styles" objects to hold lists of CSS styles. These are the JavaScript versions of CSS declarations. Each name/value pair in the object corresponds to a CSS property name and value. This is a styles object:

```
{borderWidth: '8px', borderColor: '#a0a0ff'}
```

As styles become known, they are added to an object's styles object, the object that is the value of each DOM element's property named `style`. You often want to add the properties of a new object to an existing object in the process. Listing 2-3 shows this situation in pseudo code.

Listing 2-3

```
var bstyles = borders.get_styles();
all_styles += bstyles; // pseudo code
```

The += operator does not apply to objects, but we can write a general-purpose sum function to do the same job. (We won't be able to use this general-purpose function for styles, but the one we can use for styles is even simpler. We'll get there.) As Listing 2-4 shows, a general-purpose sum() is more trouble to explain than to code.

Listing 2-4

```
sum = function (old_object, new_object) {
    var ret = {};

    for (var prop in old_object) {
            ret[prop] = old_object[prop]; }
    for (prop in new_object) {
            ret[prop] = new_object[prop]; }

    return ret;
} // end: sum()
```

This function starts by creating a new, empty object, called `ret = {}`. Then the first for/in loop copies the old object's property names and values into the new object. The second for/in loop copies the new property names and values into the new object. In the process it will create new properties as needed. It will copy just values for properties that already exist.

I invite you to try writing a sum() that preserves the original values in the event of a name conflict.

Now, let's consider styles. If delem is a DOM element, as in:

```
var delem = document.getElementById(...);
```

It is a "host object." Typically this is a C++ object that includes a property for every possible CSS property (`border`, `borderWidth`, `borderLeftWidth`, and so on). Browsers may refuse to replace host objects and they may not inform you about the problem. Try a specific-purpose function such as the one in Listing 2-5.

Listing 2-5

```
function sum_to_host(host_obj, new_obj) {

    for (var prop in new_obj) {
        host_obj[prop] = new_obj[prop];
    }

} // end: sum_to_host()
```

If every property name in new_obj is already in host_obj (and they all should be for a DOM style property) this will simply replace property values in the host object. That will be trouble-free.

OP for Inheriting Prototypes

You can also use the sum() function to copy prototypes, underneath an extends() function. The latter provides a meaningful name and saves typing, two reasons worthy of our support. Listing 2-6 shows my simple extends().

Listing 2-6

```
extends = function (extend, base) {
    extend.prototype = sum(
        extend.prototype,
        base.prototype);
}
```

This copies the base class's prototype into the extending class's prototype object. Isn't this wasteful? Yes, but not very wasteful. Remember that there is only one prototype for the family, whether that is three or three thousand objects. And none of those objects will have to look back in its prototype chains for base class properties.

OP in the JSWindows Library

For those who have not totally understood the idea (and for those who are asking, "Is it really that simple?"), we'll discuss additional examples of object programming from the JSWindows library.

DOM Related

The JSWindows library functions are divided into a "DOM related" group, for dealing with the browser's host environment, and a "Utility" group, for everything else. Almost 80% of both make use of some form of object programming. Listing 2-7 shows the function that deletes a single DOM element. This would be simpler if one browser's bugs did not make it necessary to assign null to the deleted reference. ("Delem" is a contraction of "DOM element.")

Listing 2-7

```
delete_delem = function (delem) {

    while (delem.firstChild) {
        delete_delem(delem.firstChild);
    }
    delem.parentNode.removeChild(delem);
    delem = null; // Some MSIE needs this.

} // end: delete_delem()
```

This library function doesn't really use JavaScript's extended object programming. It uses the functions provided with the DOM interface to climb around the DOM object tree.

The delete_delem() function calls itself recursively to remove children from the delem. When the children are gone (and the children's children, and so on), it removes the selected element from its parent. The delem is now out of the DOM tree and will, in due course, be garbage collected and disappear.

Except, as the comment notes in some versions of one browser. Assigning null (remember, null is an object, a JavaScript bug) is needed to make the buggy browser happy.

For a second example, Listing 2-8 shows the library function that attaches an event listener to a DOM element. As with so much DOM-related work, one of its jobs is to smooth over differences between browsers. And with so many of these differences, Internet Explorer, especially older versions, is the problem.

Listing 2-8

```
/** Add an event listener. */
listen_for = function (
        wobj, event_name, func) {
    var delem = wobj.delem;

    if (delem.addEventListener !== undefined) {
        delem.addEventListener(
                event_name, func, false); }

    else if (delem.attachEvent !== undefined) {
        delem.attachEvent(
                'on' + event_name, func); }
                // IE before 9
    else { delem['on' + event_name] = func; }
        // old school!

} // end: listen_for()
```

Again we are working with object properties, in this case, event listening methods. This function uses both dot notation and subscript notation as it falls back to progressively older ways of adding the event listener.

20

An interesting feature of this library function is that the Wobj reference (Window object, the root of our family hierarchy) is passed as an explicit parameter, Fortran style. I prefer to call these functions in the object style:

```
wobj.listen_for(event_name, func);
```

Listing 2-9 shows the method in Wobj.prototype that lets us use the preferred style.

Listing 2-9

```
Wobj.prototype.listen_for = function (
        event_name, listen_func) {

    listen_for(this, event_name,
            listen_func);
}
```

When you call object.method(), the object reference on the left is converted to the this parameter within the method. The listen_for() instance method simply puts this back into the Fortran-style parameter list, explicitly. That gives us object-style method calling for our Fortran-style library functions.

Our third, and final, example from the DOM-related library functions removes an event listener that had been added by the old-fashioned method:

```
element.onclick = click_func;
```

Listing 2-10 shows the listener-removing function.

Listing 2-10

```
/** Remove solo listener. */
    stop_listening_on = function (
            wobj, type, func) {
    var delem = wobj.delem;

    delem['on' + type] = undefined;
}
```

JavaScript's subscript notation makes this job simple.

Utility

I have been a big fan of object programming for a long time so it came as no surprise that most of the DOM-related utilities manipulated object's properties. After all, the DOM is an object tree. What I was surprised to find was how many of my utility (non-DOM) functions also used OP. Let's start with a simple example.

Whenever you write a constructor, you should also write a toString() method. It seems you always want to have a readable version of an object as you are developing. But what about your *ex nihilo* objects? The default toString() (from Object.prototype) reports that you have "[object Object]" (an object created by the Object() constructor). This is almost never helpful. Listing 2-11 shows a simple utility that creates a readable version of an object.

Listing 2-11

```
o2s = function (obj) {
    var ret = [];
    for (var pname in obj) {
        var prop = obj[pname];
        if (typeof prop !== 'function') {
            ret.push(pname + ': ' + prop);
        }
    }
    return 'object{' + ret.join(',') + '}';
}
```

This loops through the properties by their names (in pname) and, if they are not functions, pushes them onto an array of property name/value pairs, as strings. That array is used as the center of the returned string.

Note that the for/in loop looks at "enumerable" properties. This means, roughly, the properties you create, but not the administrative properties JavaScript creates. It is generally exactly what you want. ECMAScript 5 gives you precise control for the times when you need to make exceptions. (See Appendix H.)

Listing 2-12 shows an example of object programming applied to arrays. (Arrays are objects, in JavaScript.) It removes an element from an array, shortening the array by one (ensuring that there are no undefined elements created).

Listing 2-12

```
remove_element = function(arr, element) {

    var index = find_index(arr, element);
    if (index === -1) { return; }

    ret = [];
    for (var i in arr) {
        if (i !== index) { ret.push( arr[i]; )
    return ret;

} // end: remove_element()
```

One of the most common mistakes in any object programming is to assign a second reference to an object when a second object is needed.

```
var not_really_second = first;
```

When not_really_second is changed, the same change appears in first as they are both references to a single object. Making a shallow copy of first is normally correct.

```
var not_really_second = shallow_copy(first);
```

Listing 2-13 shows our shallow_copy() function.

Listing 2-13

```
shallow_copy = function (obj) {
    var ret;

    if (obj instanceof Array) { ret = []; }
    else if (obj instanceof Function) {
            ret = obj; }
    else { ret = {}; }

    for (var name in obj) {
            ret[name] = obj[name]; }

    return ret;
} // end: shallow_copy()
```

The code that copies arrays and non-array objects is identical except that the return value is initialized differently. The calling code does not care. Note that using a for/in loop to copy the array correctly handles sparse arrays and arrays that have been modified via splice() calls.

For those new to shallow and deep copying, a "shallow" copy copies references to other objects. A "deep" copy would duplicate the objects and arrays referenced. During a shallow copy, statements such as the following are executed:

```
copy.prop_name = original.prop_name;
```

This creates a second property with the same name and value as the first, but it is totally separate. After the assignment, there is no connection between the two.

If the code subsequently assigns to the copy, it does not impact the original.

```
copy.prop_name = some_other_object;
```

The above statement replaces the value of copy.prop_name with another object reference. It has no effect on the value of original.prop_name.

You are now equipped to consider inheritance in JavaScript, both class-based and prototypal. We'll take a close look at what is really meant by "inheritance" when programming with objects.

Summary

We started with a definition of unrestricted manipulation of objects that we called "object programming." A full definition showed that JavaScript provides nearly full object programming. Class-based OOP provides a limited subset of these manipulations.

JavaScript allows OOP-style use of property names as program literals and, via object subscripting, of variable property names. Examples from real systems shows both of these in use. The ability to add objects (combining two sets of property names) is invaluable when dealing, for example, with DOM CSS style objects.

In the next two chapters, we will look closely at "inheritance," which means very different things in the class-based and prototypal worlds.

CHAPTER 3

■ ■ ■

Inheritance Theory

Ready for a dose of theory? We can't code inheritance unless we know what "inheritance" means. And it mean a different things in OOP-land than it means in prototype-land.

Before discussing ways to implement inheritance, and alternatives for achieving its benefits, we have to define inheritance. As class-based inheritance involves classes, we need to define "classes" with enough rigor so that we can write some code.

When we say "object-oriented programming" or "OOP," we are not speaking of general programming using objects. We are speaking specifically of programming in a language such as Java or Visual Basic that uses the C++ style object model, correctly called "class-based" (incorrectly but commonly called "classical"). This chapter provides definitions leading up to "inheritance" in both OOP and JavaScript. You will see both implemented in JavaScript in Chapter 4.

Classes

The word "class" seems to attract multiple meanings. In education it could be a group of students (as in "class dismissed!") or it could be an educational session ("in this class, we will learn about..."). Applied to software, words should have single meanings. Unfortunately, this is not always the case. There are three definitions of "class" in OOP and JavaScript in this book:

> A class is a group of objects (we'll call it a "family") that share a common set of properties.

> In this chapter we will be looking at diagrams of classes. In our diagrams, the class is a set of properties.

> In class-based OOP, a class is the software that defines, creates, and supports a family of like objects. When speaking of OOP we'll refer to the "class software." In JavaScript, the constructor and its properties, such as the property named prototype, provide an alternative that you may also call a "class," but we won't call it that (in deference to JavaScript's Self roots).

In practical code the first definition usually means the objects created from a single constructor. You can create such families in JavaScript or any OOP-based language. A Window in JSWindows is an object created by the Window constructor (and therefore, a sibling to other members of the Window family).

The third definition applies to a C++ (or Java, VB, and many others) "class," the software that defines objects. The software that Stroustrup insists is at the heart of system design. In JavaScript, the constructor function and its properties serve this purpose. Most class-based languages also allow class software to have its own data and method properties. We will call this type of class the "class software" or an "OOP class" when speaking specifically about OOP language class software.

In a system written in Java, an object created from the constructor in Window.java would also be called an instance of the Window class, and that would be very similar to a JavaScript member of the Window family. However, the OOP class (the class software) cannot generally be manipulated during execution; it is not an object. The JavaScript constructor and its properties can be manipulated during execution and it is indisputably an object.

The class-based languages are not all the same, of course. Chapter 5 discusses the multiple inheritance of C++ and the somewhat comparable interfaces employed in Java.

Constructors

In class-based OOP there is one method in the class software that is called the "constructor." The constructor's job is to create objects, which are instances of the class (members of the family). Consider this example using a constructor to create an object instance:

```
lassie = new Dog('Lassie');
```

The "constructor" is the function named Dog that creates a new Dog-family object. Constructors are at the heart of class-based class software, such as Java modules. In JavaScript, any function may be a constructor but the convention is to name constructors with an initial capital letter and to not name any other functions that way.

In class-based languages, constructors create and return class instances (family members), often with the "new" keyword. In JavaScript, new is an operator that appears much like the same word in C++ or Java. (Chapter 9 digs deeply into JavaScript's new operator. If your interest in this book is purely I've-got-code-to-write you don't need Chapter 9. It may help, however, if your interest is I've-got-to-ace-this-job-interview. And its logic does lead to the interesting conclusion that JavaScript is less prototypal and more OOP-like than many would have you believe.)

Instance Methods

Instance methods are the verbs of object programming. Listing 3-1 shows examples.

Listing 3-1

```
dog.bark(); // "woof, woof"
sir_paul.sing(); // "Yesterday, all my..."
```

Unlike data properties, for which space is allocated for each object instance, these methods are part of the class software. (It would be extremely wasteful to repeat the same method code with every object instance.) In JavaScript, methods are normally part of the object's prototype (discussed in Chapter 1), which is the prototype property of the constructor. The bark() method would be referenced by Dog.prototype.bark.

In OOP languages, the instances' methods are normally fixed at compile time. In JavaScript, you could replace these methods during execution, delete them, or even change them into data properties. Methods can even be attached to individual objects, so your Beatle family could have results like those in Listing 3-2.

Listing 3-2

```
john.sing();    // "Lucy in the sky, with..."
paul.sing();    // "Michelle, ma belle..."
george.sing();  // "While my guitar gently..."
ringo.sing();   // "In an octopus's garden..."
```

(This result can be achieved in OOP languages. It cannot be done, however, by attaching individual methods to objects.)

Class (Family-Wide) Properties

In class-based OOP, class software modules are like objects in that they may have their own data and method properties. These are properties of the family, not of any single instance of the family.

Data

Class software may have its own named data properties. These are called "class static" values in Java. In JavaScript, properties of the constructor serve the same purpose. There is only one data value for each class data property. (There is one instance value for each object instance, whether there are zero or millions of instances.)

Methods

As with data properties, class software may also have its own methods. These operate on the class software's data properties. In JavaScript, function properties attached to the constructor can serve the same purpose.

We can now define inheritance with the help of some diagrams.

Class-Based Inheritance

I draw class families as ovals, like Venn diagrams referring to sets. These will be referring to object property names. (These do not refer to property values. The "Collie" named "Lassie" and "Snoopy" the "Beagle" are both instances of the Dog family having identical properties such as name and breed. They have different property values.)

Property Sets

We'll work with families E and B. If the properties of E are a superset of the properties of B, E extends B and B is the base class in OOP-inheritance terms.

The property names of families E and B may be disjoint (no names in common), overlapping (some names in common), or one may be a superset of the other.

Figure 3-1 shows families that share some property names.

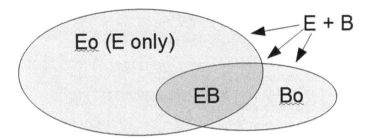

Figure 3-1.

In this example, families E and B have some property names in common (area EB) and other properties that are not shared in Eo (E only) and Bo (B only). Next, let's consider the inheritance case, where Bo is an empty set.

Figure 3-2 shows family E (Extend) having a superset of the properties of family B (Base).

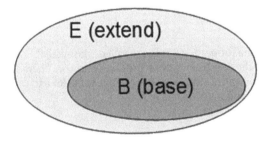

Figure 3-2.

In class-based OOP, when Bo is empty we say that E "extends" B, or E "inherits from" B. Class-based OOP designs focus on inheritance, deliberately seeking this type of family relationship. This book will show an inheritance hierarchy, such as the one in Figure 3-2, this way.

E
    B

In the E class software there would be a statement such as E extends B, in Java, or class E: B, less readable (even with access qualifiers omitted) in C++. The class software for E would then define only the extending properties, shown in Figure 3-3 as E minus B.

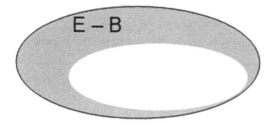

Figure 3-3.

The "hole" holds the additional properties, defined in separate class software that defines B. It is filled in when you specify that E extends B or B is "inherited" by E.

Constructing an Extending Instance

To create an instance of an extending family, the constructor of the base family, B, is executed first. The constructor of the extending family, E, then runs, adding properties. (The additional properties may require computations using the values of the base properties.)

Overriding Properties

You could create properties in family E that had the same names as properties in family B. These properties in the extending family would "override" the same-named properties in the base family. There are times, however, when you will want both. The toString() method is one common case.

A toString() method is usually programmed for every OOP or JavaScript family. This method shows the object's family name and its key property names and values. My Dog.prototype.toString() would report the following:

```
Dog{name:Lassie,breed:Collie}
```

(I usually ignore method properties in the toString() method.) These toString() methods are invaluable when debugging. When family E extends B, its base family, you want your toString() to report like this:

```
E{ B{B props} E added props }
```

That embeds the toString() of B within the toString() of E. We will, on occasions such as this, want to call overridden methods from base families. (Some OOP languages and some copycat JavaScript libraries use "super" to refer to base families. I object. In the first place, the base family is a subset, not a superset, of the extending family.

29

Additionally, using any term, even a well-chosen term such as "subset," to refer to the immediate base family does not give us access to families arbitrarily far back in an inheritance chain.)

Inheritance Chains

An extending family can be used as a base family by another extending family, this way:

F
    E
        B

Figure 3-4 illustrates this.

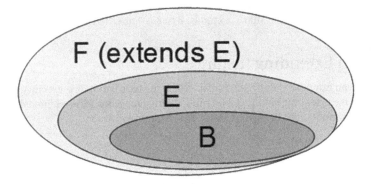

Figure 3-4.

The diagram shows that reference to "the subset" of family F is ambiguous. E and B are both subsets of F. Note that this is not multiple inheritance, shown in Figure 3-5 and discussed in Chapter 6. In multiple inheritance, there are two base families, independent of each other.

You want a toString() for F that reports:

```
F{ E{ B{B props} E added props} F added props}
```

F is built on E as its base class. E is built on B. In Chapter 4 we'll look at a technique that makes this quite easy to code.

In an inheritance chain, there are no independent base families like those you see in Figure 3-5.

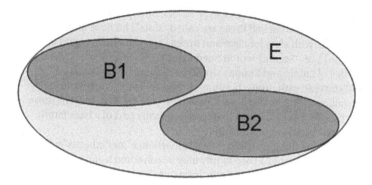

Figure 3-5.

In our JSWindows system, the Wobj (Window object) is the common ancestor of all families that place objects in the visible window of the browser. The Rect family (screen rectangles) inherits from Wobj. A basic Rect is extended, by the addition of a closing "X" button in the right-top corner, to be a Window. This is extended, in turn, by the addition of a title (it serves as a handle for dragging) and move logic to be a movable Window_M. The addition of various sizing buttons (min, max, and intermediate sizes) gives us a movable, button-sizable window: Window_M_BS. To summarize:

```
Window_M_BS
    Window_M
        Window
            Rect
                Wobj
```

Each family except Wobj extends a base. Each family except Windows_M_BS is the base for an extending family.

This is a typical example of how inheritance is designed into systems, creating progressively more complex objects by extending simpler ones. These designs, and JSWindows is no exception, are often force fitted. (Suppose you wanted a window that could be minimized, but was not movable. Sorry.) This chain also hints at how messy the inheritance chain can make methods that attempt to use overridden inherited methods. The toString() method for Window_M_BS must access each of the extended families' toString() methods. You will see that JavaScript makes this quite simple.

Prototypal Inheritance

Prototypal inheritance, pioneered in the Self language, uses the word, "inheritance," but with a different meaning. In Self objects inherit directly from each other. The base object is called the "prototype" of the inheriting object.

A Self object is said to "inherit" from its prototype object. Snoopy might inherit from Lassie. If Lassie had properties (in Self these are called "slots") for name and breed, Snoopy would start life with slots for name and breed (and the values would be, respectively, Lassie and Collie—Snoopy would need fixing).

In OOP, the properties of Lassie and Snoopy would be defined by the Dog class software. Neither would start life with property values. Commonly, the constructor would be passed these values when the Dog object instances were created. In OOP, these properties are not "inherited." Only properties that were originally part of a base family (perhaps Pet) are "inherited" by an extending family.

This book uses the OOP terminology when it says "inheritance" or "inherits" without qualification. Properties that are part of a base family may be inherited by an extending family. We do not, however, say that Snoopy inherits from Dog. In pure prototypal inheritance Snoopy might inherit from Lassie. In OOP we do not apply "inheritance" to the process of creating a new instance of a family from the family's constructor.

To put it in prototypal terms, Snoopy, when you write:

```
snoopy = new Dog(...);
```

snoopy is assigned Dog.prototype as his prototype, but we do not call this inheritance. This is mostly just a practical place to put instance method code. OOP reserves the term "inheritance" to refer, for example, to Dog extends Mammal;. Inheritance happens, in OOP, when one class creates a superset of a base class.

Inheritance vs. Composition

I do not want to seem to endorse inheritance as an architectural tool. In their classic book, *Design Patterns: Elements of Reusable Object-Oriented Software* (1995, Gamma et. al.), the Gang of Four advise us to prefer composition over inheritance. I do and you should, too.

Composition in Theory

If an object includes another type of object as a property, it is using composition. This is called the "has a" relationship. In JSWindows, each screen object could "have a" border. The border is wrapped into a Borders object.

In contrast, inheritance is used when one object "is a" object of some less complex design. In JSWindows, a Window "is a" Rect with an added closing button.

Composition in JSWindows

An onscreen object is not a simple thing. Assuming a rectangular shape, you have to consider position and size, borders and background, styles for fonts and text position and behaviors, just to name a few. In the JSWindows examples in Chapter 1, you saw three windows. The title was not a window, but it was a visible object. Listing 3-3 shows the code (a single constructor call) that was required to create the page title.

Listing 3-3

```
var h1 = new Wobj( SCREEN,
        'heading_1', 'h1',
        [10,10, 300,40],
        0,
        {backgroundColor:
            'rgba( 250, 250, 250, 0.5 )',
        fontFamily: 'Times New Roman, serif',
        fontSize: '24pt',
        margin: '10px',
        paddingLeft: '10px',
        paddingTop: '5px',
        paddingRight: '10px'},
        {innerHTML: 'JSW: JSWindows, v2'} );
```

Note that the software is carefully minimized. The remaining complexity is there because the reality (putting an object on the screen) cannot be further reduced without losing the flexibility needed.

The first three arguments specify the parent container, the title (used as an ID internally), and the type of HTML element (in this case, <h1>). The fourth argument is an array for the pos_size (position and size) object, specifying [left,top, width, height]. The fifth element, a zero, specifies the Borders object. We will take a look at Borders, but first note that we already have used composition to bring in the parent, the pos_size, and the borders.

Why use an object as a property? You do so when the object is too complex for a simple property. Complexity could come in the number of components, or in the behaviors. We'll think about each with our Borders family.

Complex Properties

A Borders object maintains the full specification of the four borders (left, top, right, and bottom) of every object to which the CSS box model applies (virtually every visible object). Three properties can be applied:

- Width

- Type (solid, dashed, groove, etc.)

- Color

Each of these can be a single value applying to all four sides, or four values, one for each side. (I didn't bother with CSS's two- and three-value alternatives.) Additionally, corner radii can be supplied. This can be as simple as a single value establishing the radius for all four corners, or it can be a single value for each corner, or a vertical/horizontal pair for each corner. (If you are counting, that's up to four values for each of width, type and color, plus up to eight values for radii: 20 possible values.)

Behaviors

For reasons I never understood (reasons that have triggered no end of expletives), the W3C box model insists that the size of an object is the size of its content area. (The area inside the padding. The padding, in turn, is inside the border.) To do any kind of layout, you normally want to know the size of the object, including borders, padding, and content. (In today's CSS, that's box-sizing: border-box;.) To make this simple (or at least to make it seem simple, from the outside) we fit out our Borders with methods such as the ones shown in Listings 3-4 and 3-5.

Listing 3-4

```
Borders.prototype.get_width_left =
        function() {

    if (this.width instanceof Array) {
            return this.width[0]; }

    return this.width;
}
```

(All objects in the JSWindows system are part of the jsw2 namespace object. These references have not been included in the listings unless they are important to understanding the code.) There are, of course, three other similar methods for the other three sides. These are then combined in methods like the one shown in Listing 3-5.

Listing 3-5

```
Borders.prototype.get_width_horizontal =
        function() {

    if (this.width instanceof Array) {
        return this.width[0] + this.width[2];
    }

    return 2 * this.width;
}
```

There is another similar method for vertical borders.

The key to using borders is to be able to output CSS styles from our specification. Outside, this is easy. You just ask:

```
... = xxx.borders.get_styles();
```

This allows you to forget that the get_styles() method weighs in at nearly 70 lines! How could something that is so simple (at least in concept) take so much code?

Listing 3-6 shows a single block extracted from the borders.get_styles() method.

Listing 3-6

```
if (borders.color !== undefined) {
    if (borders.color instanceof Array) {
        styles['borderLeftColor'] =
                borders.color[0];
        styles['borderTopColor'] =
                borders.color[1];
        styles['borderRightColor'] =
                borders.color[2];
        styles['borderBottomColor'] =
                borders.color[3];
    } else { styles['borderColor'] =
            borders.color; }
} else { styles['borderColor'] =
        DEFAULTS.Borders.color; }
```

If the border colors are specified with an array, this code uses one value at a time for borderLeftColor, borderTopColor, and so on. A single value may specify the borderColor. Or, if nothing is specified, the system uses the DEFAULTS value. Unfortunately, code can be very simple without being short.

This gives you a glimpse of the code behind the Borders family objects. I hope it has been enough to show why an object was required; a simple property or two would not be adequate.

Regardless, you should always prefer composition over inheritance, though the latter is our focus in this chapter. In Chapter 4, we'll look at the code for implementing inheritance in JavaScript.

Summary

Inheritance happens in OOP when one class, the extending class, creates a superset of a base class. The objects in the extending class family will have the properties (data and method) of the base plus additional properties added by the extending class.

In prototypal inheritance one object is given the same properties (data and method) of another object. A family is created if several objects inherit from one "prototypal" object.

Our Dog() constructor creates objects in the Dog family. This is called "inheritance" in the prototypal model. Creating objects from an OOP constructor is not called "inheritance."

In practice we will put method code in our prototype and data properties in individual family members. The technique of creating objects explained in Chapter 1 has all our Dog family objects sharing a single prototype, Dog.prototype, but is otherwise most similar to the OOP model.

Enough! Theory is only useful if it helps us write code. Chapter 4 returns to the world of coding.

CHAPTER 4

■ ■ ■

Inheritance Practice

In this chapter we get back to coding. We'll look at the practical steps you need to take to make OOP-style inheritance work, using JavaScript as Eich designed it.

When family E extends B, an instance of E has some of its own data and method properties, and it acquires the data and method properties of family B. Instance data properties are commonly assigned by the constructor and instance methods are commonly made available in the prototype. In this chapter you'll see how JavaScript— plain JavaScript, library functions not required—can successfully use its hybrid class/ prototypal object model to create class-based OOP inheritance hierarchies. These do not require, and do not really want, JavaScript's prototype chain.

I do not recommend inheritance-based architecture; I just want to demonstrate, for the benefit of veterans of class-based OOP languages, that it is simple to create inheritance hierarchies in JavaScript.

Cascading `init()` Methods for Data

If you cannot use the base family's constructor, how can you achieve inheritance of data properties? There is a simple solution: moving the logic out of the constructor into methods that you write. For the initialization code, you write methods named `Xxx.init()` (where Xxx is the name of the constructor). They do whatever you tell them to do, leaving JavaScript constructors to handle the assignment of prototypes and nothing more. If you were creating a dog with a constructor such as the one in Listing 4-1.

Listing 4-1

```
function Dog(name, breed) {
    var new_dog = this;

    new_dog.name = name;
    new_dog.breed = breed;
}
```

You would change that to the two functions in Listing 4-2.

Listing 4-2

```
function Dog(name, breed) {
    var new_dog = this;
    Dog.init(new_dog, name, breed);
}
Dog.init = function(new_dog, name, breed) {
    new_dog.name = name;
    new_dog.breed = breed;
}
```

You'll see how this enables inheritance in a moment. More generally, if the parameters needed by family B are b1, b2, and so on, the init() looks like Listing 4-3.

Listing 4-3

```
function B(b1, b2, ...) {
    var new_b = this;

    B.init(new_b, b1, b2, ...);
}

B.init = function(new_b, b1, b2, ...) {
    new_b.b1 = b1;
    new_b.b2 = b2;
    ...
}
```

Function B() is a constructor, to be used after the new operator. This function (by rather complex "magic" explained in Chapter 9) makes B.prototype the prototype object for each instance it creates. B.init() is a reference to a non-constructor function. (As a property of B(), it is like an OOP class (family-wide) method. Instance methods would be properties of B.prototype.)

When the calling code creates an instance of the B family, nothing is changed.

```
var b = new B(b1, b2, ...);
```

However, the logic is all external to the constructor, available to an extending family's constructor. Why the extra trouble? If you put the constructor logic in an init() method, an extending class can use it.

The highlighted line in Listing 4-4 shows the call to B.init() from an extending E.init().

Listing 4-4

```
function E(b1, b2, e1, e2, ...) {
    var new_e = this;
    E.init(new_e, b1, b2, e1, e2 ...)
}

E.init = function(new_e, b1, b2, e1, e2, ...) {
    B.init(new_e, b1, b2);
    new_e.e1 = e1;
    new_e.e2 = e2;
    ...
}
```

Here the E (extending) family's constructor logic (in E.init()) starts by calling its base family's constructor logic (in B.init()).

Note that B.init() and E.init() are not constructors. They are properties of constructor functions. In OOP, these would be family-wide methods. Note also that a family that extends E will not even need to know that E extends B. Simply calling E.init() will be enough. Whether E stands on its own or extends a long chain of other families will not matter.

A Theoretical Example

The "Master Classers" link on my website takes you to inheritance code from Crockford, Edwards, Flanagan, and Resig. That code is compared to using plain JavaScript. I show the plain JavaScript solution here. A family hierarchy is proposed: C extends B and B extends A.

```
C
    B
        A
```

The ability to run overridden methods of extended families is tested by requiring the toString() of family C to access the toString() of family B which, in turn, accesses the toString() of family A.

The A constructor assigns, through A.init(), two parameters to properties of the base family, as Listing 4-5 shows.

Listing 4-5

```
function A(p1, p2) {
    A.init(this, p1, p2);
}

A.init = function (new_a, p1, p2) {
    new_a.a = p1;
    new_a.b = p2;
}
```

```
A.prototype.toString = function () {
    return 'A{' +
        'a=' + this.a +
        ',b=' + this.b +
    '}';
}
```

Note that the value of the parameter new_a (the object being created) in the init() method is the value of the this pseudo-parameter of the constructor. In a function executed on the right side of the new operator, this will be a reference to the new object being built.

Let's look at how family B extends A. The B() constructor has four parameters, the first two for the base family, A, and the next two for the extending family, B. It also has a method, toString(), that overrides the method of the same name in the base family. This was deliberately complicated by the requirement that the toString() of the extending family had to access the toString() method that it overrode. Listing 4-6 shows that this does not require a lot of code.

Listing 4-6

```
function B(p1, p2, p3, p4) {
    B.init(this, p1, p2, p3, p4);
}
B.init = function (new_b, p1, p2, p3, p4) {
    A.init(new_b, p1, p2);
    new_b.c = p3;
    new_b.d = p4;
}
B.prototype.toString = function () {
    return 'B{' +
        A.prototype.toString.call(this) +
        ',c=' + this.c +
        ',d=' + this.d +
    '}';
}
```

The B.init() method passes the first two calling parameters to A.init(). Code that uses an instance of B can use b.p1 or b.p3 to address the data properties, without caring that p1 is a base family property and p3 is an extending family property. The toString() method of an instance of B can be called for a readable report, as Listing 4-7 shows.

Listing 4-7

```
var b = new B(1,2,3,4);
b.toString(); // "B{A{a=1,b=2},c=3,d=4}"
```

I was never happy that the toString() of the extending family relied on the call() function method, but I used it regardless.

The `call()` and `apply()` Methods

There are two seldom used and little known JavaScript methods that can be used on functions: `call()` and `apply()`. They do the same thing. They let the programmer take over from JavaScript and assign directly to the `this` parameter used inside a function. I avoid these methods if at all possible because I doubt the maintenance programmer who "inherits" my code after I have moved on will be familiar with them. However, they are needed, on occasion.

To use a function that has no explicit parameters with a custom value for `this`, use `call()`.

```
any_func.call(value_for_this);
```

The function will be called and `this`, inside the function, will be assigned the value you specified. (Using `call()` can be a lifesaver. JavaScript does not always supply the value you need for `this`.)

If the function you want to call has one or two explicit parameters (for example, `p1`, `p2`), you precede them with your `this` value:

```
any_func.call(value_for_this, p1, p2);
```

The `call()` method (it is a method in `Function.prototype`, so you can use it on any function) will pass along any return value, so you can write:

```
var ret = any_func.call(value_for_this);
```

You can use `call()` (for lack of a good alternative) to get direct access to overridden `toString()` methods, for example. In Listing 4-8, E extends B.

Listing 4-8

```
E.prototype.toString = function () {
    return 'E{' +
        b.prototype.toString.call(this) +
        // E's other properties here
    '}';
}
```

The `apply()` function works the same way, except that it provides for a list of parameters of unspecified length. Look it up if you need it; avoid it if you can.

Extending an Extending Family

The last requirement of our theoretical example was to show that a third family could extend the extending family, without knowing or caring that its base family was extending another base. Listing 4-9 shows that it meets this requirement.

Listing 4-9

```
function C(p1, p2, p3, p4, p5, p6) {
    C.init(this, p1, p2, p3, p4, p5, p6);
}
C.init = function (inst, p1, p2,
        p3, p4, p5, p6) {
    B.init(inst, p1, p2, p3, p4);
    inst.e = p5;
    inst.f = p6;
}
C.prototype.toString = function () {
    return 'C{' +
        B.prototype.toString.call(this) +
        ',e=' + this.e +
        ',f=' + this.f +
    '}';
}
```

Here you see the first four (of six) data values passed to `B.init()` where B will be initialized. C neither knows nor cares about other classes that B extends. The final two data values will be assigned as C's extending properties. C will neither know nor care how its base family assigns the first four values.

Similarly, C will use B's `toString()` to report on the four values that it let B handle. The report will be exactly the one you want, as Listing 4-10 shows.

Listing 4-10

```
var c = new C(1,2,3,4,5,6);
alert(c);
// "C{B{A{p1=1,p2=2},p3=3,p4=4},p5=5,p6=6}"
```

Since using this technique as a baseline to compare against the inheritance library alternatives of Edwards, Flanagan, and Resig, I have used it regularly. The JSWindows system is one example. I deliberately pushed the JavaScript philosophy (keep inheritance chains short) aside in favor of a long, OOP-style inheritance hierarchy, but the technique showed no problems.

A Practical Example

In the JSWindows system, the `Wobj` (Window OBJect) is the base of the hierarchy of onscreen families.

```
Window_M_BS
    Window_M
        Window
            Rect
                Wobj
```

(This cascade is a simplification. Button also extends Rect, for example. Button_close extends Button and so on.)

Listing 4-11 is the code in the Window_M_BS constructor. The one line needed to inherit from Window_M is highlighted.

Listing 4-11

```
Window_M_BS = function (...params...) {
    Window_M_BS.init(this, ...params...);
}


Window_M_BS.init = function (new_window,
        ...params...) {

    Window_M.init(new_window, ...params...);

    // sizing button logic here
}
```

Similarly, Window_M.init() will call Window.init(). Window.init() will call Rect.init(). Rect.init() will call Wobj.init(). Every constructor moves its logic into an init() method, and each init() starts by calling the init() for the family it extends.

That technique shows all the code, save for the details. The devil, as they say in politics, is in the details. With JSWindows, the devil was in the default values.

Discrete Defaults

I use a SKIN object that the designer can use to tailor colors, sizes, and other cosmetics to his or her own designs. Much of the hierarchy can be styled separately. For example, the basic window object, the Wobj, gets a two-pixel, solid border. Window objects get a wider, ridge border. At each step the system checks to see if a style has been explicitly specified. If not, it uses the default styles.

Listing 4-12 shows an example from the Window family.

Listing 4-12

```
if (borders === undefined) {
    borders = new Borders(
        DEFAULTS.Window.border_width,
        DEFAULTS.Window.border_style,
        // etc.
```

The code goes on to add border colors and radii. As a convenience it allows the border width to be specified, and lets the other values default, so the default borders block is followed by a similar one that checks to see if borders is a number and then assigns the other defaults. This is not rocket science, but it does amount to quite a bit of code.

Implementing Capabilities

The init() methods in JSWindows follow this pattern:

1. Set defaults.

2. Call the base family's init().

3. Add logic.

The logic added includes assigning parameters to properties (object.property = parameter;). If the names are well-chosen, the parameter name and the property name may be the same. Then any new capabilities are added. This can be very simple. A Window is a Rect that is Closable (has a closing "X" button, right-top corner). This is the entire logic needed to implement that capability.

```
new_window.implement('Closable');
```

(Of course, the Closable capability had to be programmed. Figuring out how to place an "X" in a small Rect—matching font points to button pixels—took some work. Otherwise, it was simple.)

Sometimes, a small bit of code is required. For example, our window sizing buttons include min and max with three sizes in between. The in-between sizes are named, not creatively, 0, 1, and 2. By default, if the button_choices argument is not supplied, you get all five buttons, as Listing 4-13 shows.

Listing 4-13

```
if (button_choices === undefined) {
    button_choices =
        ['min', '0', '1', '2', 'max']; }

    new_window.implement(
        'Button_sizable', button_choices);
```

Next we'll leave the constructors and init() methods that provide data property inheritance to look at method property inheritance.

Prototypes for Methods

To have the benefits of class-based inheritance, you need to do the equivalent of placing the instance method code in the class software. In JavaScript, with its hybrid class/prototypal model, that means putting the methods into the prototype. (We'll also consider alternatives after we see what is required to use the prototype.)

Theory

In Self, objects "inherit" from a prototype object. The arguments in favor of this approach very much resemble the arguments in favor of agile programming. In class-based OOP, considerable effort is required to design the family hierarchies before coding begins. Experienced designers report the same thing: the design is never right. This is no reflection on the skill of the designers. Unanticipated relationships appear between families. Inheritance doesn't work because the subset/superset relationship doesn't hold. Multiple base families appear where the design tried to avoid multiple inheritance. The code often requires revision deep into its earliest families (families on which the rest of the system has grown to depend). Refactoring is never as easy as one hopes.

By contrast, the prototypal advocates assert, the way to get started is to create an object that meets your immediate needs, use it as a prototype, and build something. You want to get to the point where you start discovering those troubling relationships between your families without having a lot of code already depending on the original design.

In my experience, very few systems contradict the theory that "the design is never right." You learn more by building a system. What you learn usually becomes what you wish you had known when you started. Carefully designed hierarchies generally need refactoring. Does it follow that the prototypal approach is best? Not necessarily. Sometimes a quick prototype is a very helpful learning tool that gets you pointed in the right direction. (It's good to find the right direction when there's still so little code that starting over is no problem.) Sometimes a quick prototype leads you into a trap, but you won't see it until you've "completed" half or more of the system. (Remember what Brooks said. "Plan to throw one away. You will, anyhow." Frederick P. Brooks, Jr., *The Mythical Man-Month*, 1972.) By way of proving that some things never change, if you look at my source code you'll see the namespace name is jsw2. If you're guessing that the original was named jsw, you're right.

JavaScript lets you design hierarchies or just make a quick prototype. It is completely agnostic on the subject. The ability to use object programming (Chapter 2) and to substitute capabilities for family hierarchies (Chapter 6) will certainly help, whichever approach you take.

Prototypal Inheritance

Pure prototypal inheritance is easy to code in JavaScript, although the code is cryptic. The commonly recommended solution, if family E extends family B, is shown in Listing 4-14.

Listing 4-14

```
E.init = function(new_e, args) {...}

E.prototype = new B(args B needs);

E.prototype.another_func = function ...
```

You assign an object of family B to E.prototype. Then you add the E-specific functions to E.prototype. You have used an instance of B as the prototype for instances of E.

Now, JavaScript will look to E.prototype for properties of an E instance that it doesn't find in the object. And it will look to the prototype of E.prototype (its value is B.prototype) for properties not found in E.prototype. This "inherits" the unknown properties from B. At best, this is sub-optimal.

The properties of B commonly include data and methods. You seldom want data properties that are the same for every object instance. (If you use Lassie as a prototype, you probably don't want Snoopy's breed to be "Collie," even temporarily.) You will probably assign values to your new E object that you pass in as arguments to the constructor. If these replace all the B data properties then the B data properties will be merely wasting space in E.prototype. This is inelegant but likely immaterial. The problem is the properties that are not overridden.

Assume you want all instances of E to share data values. A better approach is to assign these shared values to the E constructor.

```
E.shared_property = shared_value;
```

The code will then refer to E.shared_property, making it clear that this is a value shared by all instances, not an instance property. (And it will also eliminate the "didn't find it, look it up in the prototype" step an instance variable would require.)

The conclusion is that assigning a B instance to E.prototype is not the best way to inherit data properties from B. What about methods?

Assume that B's methods were stored in B.prototype. Assigning an instance of B to E.prototype gives instances of E access to these methods, in two lookup steps. An instance of E needs to execute, for example, b_method(). The code specifies e_inst.b_method(). JavaScript does not find a b_method property of e_inst, so it looks in E.prototype. Again, it doesn't find b_method, so it looks in the prototype of E.prototype (B.prototype), where it will find the method it needs.

These lookups are fast, but they should still be avoided if they aren't helpful. Can we do better?

Prototype Inheritance Alternatives

Performance is optimized if you assign references to the inherited methods (in B.prototype) to names in E.prototype, as Listing 4-15 shows.

Listing 4-15

```
E.prototype.b_meth0 = B.prototype.b_meth0;
E.prototype.b_meth1 = B.prototype.b_meth1;
...
```

This approach requires a bit more programming effort and may be a maintenance issue. (Will this list of inherited method properties be updated when you add a new method to B?) A small object programming function (see Chapter 2) could automate the necessary updates.

Another approach, and the easiest way to get all methods in B.prototype into E.prototype, is to simply assign a reference.

```
E.prototype = B.prototype;
```

That is easy, but it has one major problem. If you override any method in E.prototype, the method will also change in B.prototype. As you will almost certainly want E.prototype.toString() to be more extensive than B.prototype.toString(), you need something better.

JSWindows uses a library function, extends(), to add B.prototype to E.prototype.

```
extends(E, B);
```

The extends() utility function is a typing-saving way of calling our utility, sum(). (Remember sum()? It was the OP sample that you couldn't really use for the style host object. We don't have a host object here.) sum() adds the methods in B.prototype to E.prototype. Since the methods that we say are "in B.prototype" are, in fact, references to methods, not the methods themselves, this is exactly what you want. If you want to make a unique version of an inherited method, a new reference will replace the one you need to upgrade.

```
E.prototype.toString = function ...
```

This will not affect the method of the same Inheritance practice:prototype:name in B.prototype. (The function on the right, above, is somewhere in memory. A reference to that function is assigned to the left of the equals sign, to the toString property of the prototype property of the object E. That has no impact on anything in the object B.)

Listing 4-16 shows the technique used in JSWindows, combining init() methods for data inheritance and object summing for method inheritance.

Listing 4-16

```
Function E(params) {
    var new_e = this;
    E.init(new_e, params);
}
E.init = function(new_e, params) {...}

extends(E, B);

E.prototype.another_func = function ...
```

Note that this is the same logic as in Listing 4-14, except that the highlighted line now sums the prototypes, rather than assigning an instance of the base family. Our execution speed is improved, and perhaps more important, our code readability is dramatically improved. JSWindows uses class-based inheritance; it does not use the prototype chain.

Prototype Alternatives

We are still using the prototype, and a single prototype lookup, to access instance methods. You would save CPU cycles by eliminating this lookup (although I doubt it would be enough cycles to have any impact on the user's perception of application performance). Do you have choices?

Library Functions

Going all the way back to Fortran, in the 1950s, we could use the granddaddy of all patterns: the function library. The object method calling syntax is:

```
object.method(args);
```

The equivalent library function call is:

```
method(object, args);
```

For any one method, there's very little difference. If you simply prefer the object syntax, well, I do too. And the object syntax lets us reuse one method name for each object family (subtype polymorphism through dynamic binding, if you like details—duck.talk() may be a different method than cow.talk(), if you like animals).

Prototype Lookups and Performance

Let's consider performance for a moment.

In a visual application (on a monitor, tablet, phone, or whatever), "instant" response means "in time for the next screen refresh." Monitors generally refresh 60 times per second. Smaller devices are often faster. At 1GHz (a speed that became the low-end standard in smart phones in 2011), your viewer's CPU clock ticks about 17 million times between screen refreshes. A prototype lookup may waste a hundred or even a thousand of those clock ticks. Can you afford to waste a lookup? The answer is obviously "yes" if you are talking about a single lookup. The answer becomes less obvious when you are talking about multiple lookups in an inheritance chain, and multiple inheritance chains (possibly several for every object on the screen) in a single draw operation.

Consider three windows in the JSWindows system. Three objects on the screen? Well, there are three windows. But each has a title (another object on the screen). Each has three to five sizing buttons (each another object on the screen). Each window has a closing button. Those sample windows are five to seven objects, each, and they are demo windows, without content. Think about creating medium-sized dialog boxes. You quickly find a very large number of objects on the screen.

Class (Family-Wide) Methods

Another alternative is to use family-wide methods, not instance methods. This is, in fact, just another way of organizing library functions. Whether you place these functions in a Fortran-style library, append them in groups to pseudo-objects like JavaScript's Math object, or address them as OOP class methods (constructor properties, in JavaScript) makes no difference, except to the maintainability of the code.

In general, functions that are specific to a single family are often best organized as family-wide functions, gathered in a single place in the source and accessed with a single prefix (like Math.round, Math.ceil and so on).

Using family-wide methods is the best approach, but only when the method applies to the whole family. Methods that individual instances perform are best placed in the prototype.

JSWindows Inheritance

JavaScript in general, and JSWindows is no exception, still makes extensive use of Fortran-style libraries. (jQuery is the most popular JavaScript library, and with good reason.) Support functions, such as the extends() function used for prototype adding in JSWindows, are still well-organized this way.

JSWindows also makes occasional use of family-wide methods and regular use of the prototype as a place to store instance methods.

But I do not recommend JSWindows as a model for your work. It was deliberately created with an excess of inheritance as a demonstration system. In the next chapter, we will look at alternatives to inheritance.

Summary

Here we looked at the nuts and bolts of programming class-based inheritance in JavaScript. The JavaScript constructor following the new operator creates prototypes automatically, but that complicates your life when you need to have one class extend another class. We got around this problem by taking all the logic out of the constructor, and putting it in an init() method so we could call Base.init() from the Extend() constructor.

Method code is assigned directly to the constructors' prototype properties, where it will not be repeated in every instance object.

Next we'll go on to look at other principles behind object-oriented programming. If you thought there were three main principles, you'll be pleased to see that there are, indeed, three main principles.

CHAPTER 5

■ ■ ■

On OOP Principles

Here we take another break from coding to look at the principles of OOP in theory. JavaScript supports most of them very nicely.

> *According to the principles of object-oriented programming, all OOP languages have three traits in common: encapsulation, polymorphism, and inheritance.*

—Subhasis Nayak

This declaration is typical in discussion of OOP's main principles or concepts. Encapsulation, polymorphism, and inheritance have been cited as the "big three" as commonly as any. In Wikipedia's excellent article on OOP, one section is devoted to the foolishness of picking any three characteristics of OOP in this manner (and we agree). But Nayak is correct, if one is looking for the three most commonly cited features.

Ranking OOP Principles

I asked Google for its first 20 entries on "object-oriented principles." From its list I removed duplicates and those sources that did not clearly enumerate principles. Fourteen lists were left. The principles, in order of frequency of citation, are:

1. Inheritance (12 of 14 cite inheritance)

2. Encapsulation and polymorphism (11 each)

4. Classes (8)

5. Abstraction (7)

6. Interfaces (5)

7. Composition (3)

8. Cohesion, abstract classes, coupling, and messages (2)

12. Aggregation, association, components, delegation, dynamic dispatch, events, modularity, overloading, overriding, packages, properties, recursion, and specialization (1)

(For the source lists, with links, see Appendix A.)

Note that a Google-based survey assesses popularity, not importance. (You hope that there is a correlation.)

In this chapter we'll look carefully at the "big three," and at the other OOP concepts to see how JavaScript's object programming capabilities address the same needs.

Inheritance

A lot of this book is been directed specifically at inheritance, class-based and prototypal. (In our survey of OOP concepts, prototypal techniques received exactly zero citations, from which fact you are free to draw your own conclusions.) We feel it unarguable that JavaScript's choice of inheritance types and support for both class-based and prototypal models is generally superior to the class-based languages' support (or Self's support) of just one "inheritance." Let's talk about the other principles.

Encapsulation

An object can "encapsulate" information. One common technique is to provide access to the object's data properties through object methods. In Java, for example, data properties might be declared `private` while getter and setter methods (accessors and mutators, if you prefer) are declared `public`.

This lets an object hide details that are not relevant and expose only information that is needed by the outside. In U.S. life insurance, for example, a customer's "insurable age" means "age at the nearest birthday." (An infant becomes one year old at six months, two years old after 18 months, and so on.) A `public get_age()` method could return the appropriate result, without revealing the details of the computation. If the algorithm for insurable age were to change (due to changes in the law, for example), there is only one routine that needs to be updated. External systems do not access the private properties (such as date of birth).

Access Specifiers

Most class-based OOP languages have keywords that specify access permissions. Java, for example provides `private`, `protected`, and `public` as well as default (also called "package private") access. The trend has been to eliminate terminology that suggests these somehow provide data security. They don't. (The choice of the word "protected" was a mistake.)

If Mallory (the security expert's universal bad guy) has access to your system's source code, he will simply change `private` to `public` and then work his mischief. The hope is that your well-intentioned programmers, not Mallory, will work within the object's intended design, accessing properties through appropriate access methods.

JavaScript has no access specifiers. A convention has been adopted, although not universally, that a property name starting with an underscore character is private, not to be accessed. (Methods will provide the needed access to the private properties.) Any such convention requires management support to ensure that it is known and respected throughout an organization. In some environments, this is inadequate.

Closures

The JavaScript solution to provide true access limitation may be to wrap private properties in "closures," bundles of a primary function with other functions and variables. The variables in a closure are not accessible except to the functions in the closure.

The mechanics of closures are well covered in other JavaScript literature. (See Appendix F for an example.) They are not, however, a tool for JavaScript beginners. It takes a higher level of JavaScript programming skill to wrap values in closures and to maintain the code that does so. One has to weigh, as always, costs and benefits.

We conclude that other languages are better at encapsulation than JavaScript. If closures are needed, they are available, but they are not free.

Polymorphism

There are two good reasons to learn the meaning of polymorphism. First, using such a fancy word in casual conversation makes you sound intelligent. Second, polymorphism provides one of the most useful programming techniques of the object-oriented paradigm.

—*Objects and Java,* by Bill Venners

Morpheus was the God of Dreams, the one with the amazing ability of appearing in dreams of mortals in any form.

—The God of Dreams, Greek mythology

Unlike encapsulation, which has a reasonably well-agreed purpose, polymorphism has no single agreed meaning, except that of the word origin. *Poly,* many, and *morph,* from the Greek—as in the god Morpheus—means shape or form. Commonly used in biology for species with multiple appearances (tadpoles become frogs, caterpillars become butterflies). Unfortunately, the word, in computer science, has itself become polymorphic, supporting many meanings.

One source identifies four types of polymorphism: subtype, parametric, ad hoc, and coercion. We'll discuss these here.

Subtype Polymorphism

Bill Venners, writing in Objects and Java, says polymorphism is

> The ability to treat an object of any subclass of a base class
> as if it were an object of the base class. A base class has,
> therefore, many forms: the base class itself, and any of its
> subclasses.

(Remember that "subclass" is commonly used to refer to what we call an "extending" class. Also, it is common in writing about "polymorphism" to write about subtype polymorphism, ignoring other types.)

Assume you have a base type, Animal, with extending types for Cats and Cows:

```
cat.speak(); // "Meow, meow"
cow.speak(); // "Moo, moo."
```

The speak() method of the Animal classes returns a result appropriate to the type of animal. We are using speak() polymorphically. Each extending class provides an appropriate version of the method. Each object gives an appropriate result.

There are many ways to achieve this result. The polymorphic method could be defined, in C++, as a virtual method in a virtual base class. It could be defined, in Java, in an interface implemented by the extending classes. In JavaScript, the method may be defined in each extending class's prototype.

The most common example in the literature is the Shape class, which is extended by classes for Square, Circle, Triangle, and so on. The polymorphic method area() is implemented appropriately in the extending classes. See Webopedia for a typical example.

One of the grandest sounding words in object jargon is polymorphism. The essence of polymorphism is that it allows you to avoid writing an explicit conditional when you have objects whose behavior varies depending on their types.

—SourceMaking

This is another example where "polymorphism" clearly means "subtype polymorphism." Your code simply says object.area() and the area() method appropriate to the object is used. If your application has an array of Shape objects, you can compute the total area by looping through them, adding each Shape's area() to the total. Without polymorphism, the body of your loop would be a switch with one case for squares, another for circles, and so on.

See these additional links for subtype polymorphism in your favorite language: C++, Java, or C#. (The C# docs, from Microsoft, also state, "Polymorphism is often referred to as the third pillar of object-oriented programming, after encapsulation and inheritance.") There is no shortage of agreement among those who choose a "big three" that this is one of them.

While most C++-based discussion focuses on extending base classes, often virtual base classes, Java interfaces are discussed for that language (and sometimes discussed with considerable wit). One college course stresses the interface's ability to avoid implementation details.

Parametric Polymorphism

Although there is disagreement about the implementations, there is no disagreement about the terminology when we get to "parametric polymorphism."

In C++, templates can be written that describe methods that may be applied to multiple underlying types.

In Java, a similar mechanism allows for "generic" programming. You can provide functions that apply to Lists, and apply these, polymorphically, to ArrayLists and all other Java list types.

Other languages, such as C#, provide similar functionality although in different ways.

In these examples, each language supports parametric polymorphism as an advanced capability, where it will be seen less commonly than subtype polymorphism. When you get to our "capabilities" (Chapter 7), I invite you to consider adding parametric polymorphism. It needs more thinking than code.

Ad Hoc and Other Polymorphism

Forms of polymorphism that go beyond subtype and parametric are often called "ad hoc" polymorphism. You should be aware that there is widespread disagreement about what to name these types of polymorphism, and even whether they actually should be called polymorphism.

A function that works over many different types of arguments may be called polymorphic, as this Haskell source asserts.

Operators that are overloaded to support multiple operand types may be called polymorphic, as this C++ source asserts.

Functions that have different signatures (parameter lists) may be called polymorphic, as this Java source asserts.

Our original list of polymorphism types included "coercion," by which the author specifically referred to Java casts. To think about this, go back to first principles. If a method adds a foo and a bar property, it will return a result (not guaranteed to be sensible, but at least guaranteed to be a result) when applied to any object that has a foo and bar property that can be added. (Assume that "added" means "can be used on opposite sides of a plus operator.")

If a base class has a foo and a bar property, any extending class will also have those properties and can also provide a result for any function that uses those properties. However, there is no law that says our base and extending classes are the only ones that can have foo and bar properties. Myriad, seemingly unrelated, classes may have these properties. A function that adds foo and bar will produce a result as long as its object has foo and bar. Therefore this function can be applied to any object with foo and bar properties. Some will call this polymorphic.

In Java, the compiler happily accepts an extending type when a base type is required. By using a cast, the programmer tells the compiler, "use this type, too. I know what I'm doing. Trust me." As in other areas of life, such trust is sometimes justified. Using functions of mismatched types via casting may be called polymorphism. One source called it coercion polymorphism.

JavaScript and Polymorphism

Now that we agree on what polymorphism is (or at least can share an enumeration of some of the things that might be called polymorphic), we can look at how JavaScript enjoys its benefits. In a word, "fully."

When speaking of subtype polymorphism, no language has a richer set of choices for making cows say "moo" while cats say "meow." (Or for computing the areas of Shapes, if you prefer.)

Place a generic function in the base class prototype. If there is no more sensible default, have the base class method return undefined. (Or, save yourself the trouble. If there is no base function, JavaScript's prototype chain lookups will return undefined on their own.)

Override the base method with more specific methods in each extending class's prototype. Or let the base class return an instance's saying property. If Fish have nothing to say:

```
Fish.prototype.saying = function() {
        return ''; }
```

If Worms have a similar vocabulary:

```
Worm.prototype.saying = Fish.prototype.saying;
```

(You will not do this if there is even a remote possibility that fish and worms might have different sayings, of course. It might be better to give them separate methods even at the risk of repeating yourself.)

Classes, Abstraction, and Interfaces

For the "big three" object concepts, we decidedly prefer JavaScript's inheritance, as it lets you choose between class-based and prototypal. We prefer class-based access specifiers for enforcing encapsulation. (They may not be better, but they are easier.) And we love JavaScript's flexibility when it comes to polymorphism's main form. Now we look at the second trio of commonly cited object concepts.

Classes

Before we start on classes, note again that "objects" (or "instances") were discarded when our source lists included them. Calling "objects" one of the most important concepts in programming with objects seemed redundant. Classes, however, were not redundant.

Unfortunately, none of the eight lists that included classes even mentioned the fact that some languages have objects, but do not have classes. A reader would get the impression that classes are somehow necessary to programming with objects. Clearly, as Self and now JavaScript show, you can dispense with the classes but retain the objects, so the discussion of classes as an OOP principle is highly suspect, to say the least.

On the other hand, this book has gone to some length to explain how JavaScript's constructors, including their attached prototype properties, are functionally equivalent to the class-based languages' classes. The question isn't whether JavaScript has classes; the question is whether you choose to use the word "class" in two slightly different ways, one of which is broad enough to cover JavaScript constructors.

Clearly, JavaScript has class functionality. We will all be broad minded about letting each other choose word meanings. As engineers, we'll use JavaScript's constructors to create objects, JavaScript's `constructor.prototype` to store method code, and so on.

Abstraction

Seven of our fourteen lists include abstraction. What do they mean?

The term "abstraction" is commonly applied during the design phase when base classes are being discussed. It refers to the simplification process that goes from specifics toward fundamental class definitions.

Our business has "customers." What do we mean by that? What are the fundamental principles of customers? A law office serving customers will have a deeper understanding of the individuals involved than will, for instance, a fast-food restaurant. To the former, a customer has phone number(s), e-mail address(es), and so on. To the latter, the customer's individual data is irrelevant.

A JavaScripter should avoid abstraction, not because it is an unimportant concept, but because a semi-prototypal language has no use for long inheritance chains, and therefore no use for the kind of deep thinking involved in designing class hierarchies.

Maybe. Designing with inheritance as a key tool, in class-based languages, is a well-understood topic. C++ is into its fourth decade as this is written. JavaScript's "capabilities" are mere babies by comparison. What important principles will emerge as JavaScript-specific designs grow up? There may be another way of looking at abstraction.

Interfaces

Java's interfaces were originally presented as a poor man's alternative to multiple inheritance. Today they are vastly more important, and multiple inheritance is almost forgotten. (Interfaces were cited by five of our fourteen lists. Multiple inheritance: zero.)

The classic "Gang of Four" book tells us to code to interfaces, not implementations. In Java, the interface is a rigorous description of the properties, sometimes data and almost always methods, that are available outside an object. An implementation is a specific class that implements the interface. The GoF advice, if followed, has us using the interface in the way it was designed, not the way it was implemented.

A specific class may be very badly written. It might be large, slow, and/or buggy. If we code to the interface, the day will come when someone rewrites the class so that it is small, fast, and elegant. Our code, if it was written to the interface, is unchanged.

(Well, that's the theory. In fact, the programmer who discovers the small, fast, elegant core will probably also discover that the interface needs some tweaking, too, and so will our code. Those changes are still likely to be much easier for us if we program to the interface.)

Interfaces, in JavaScript, are likely to exists as documentation, not code. Good documentation is worth its weight in gold, in JavaScript, or class-based code. Documenting the API before writing code is a good idea in any language. (Your software Apress.com/9781484217863 includes extensive API documentation for the JSWindows system.)

Other OOP Principles

Of the remaining principles in our lists, composition gets the most citations (3). It has already received two major citations in this book. One more citation: the GoF tell us to prefer composition over inheritance. That is one of their two major non-pattern recommendations.

Of the remaining principles in the two citation group, messaging deserves some comment. Messaging (or message passing) was a key feature of the Smalltalk object system. It simply did not catch on. (Every language supports some form of function calling. Would you accept this as a form of "messaging"?) Most OOP practitioners seem to live happily without Smalltalk's messages.

In the one-citation category we find association and aggregation. These are specific types of composition. (Perhaps they should be added to composition's total.) If they help you prefer composition over inheritance, use them.

Several of the remaining one-citation principles owe their entire support to the Wikipedia article. Sorry to say, this article is not very good at picking the leading principles of object-oriented programming. A thorough edit would help.

Summary

With a single exception—encapsulation—JavaScript excels at the principles said to underlie object-oriented programming. Do you suppose that giving an object a property named "private" and attaching any private values to it would help? Some experimenting along these lines seems in order.

CHAPTER 6

▨ ▨ ▨

More *Ex Nihilo* Objects

The more you write JavaScript, the more indispensable *ex nihilo* objects become. It seems that almost every senior JavaScript coder (senior by years of experience in JavaScript, not in life) uses *ex nihilo* objects as namespaces, which we'll look at first. I claim a bit more originality for the idea of an *ex nihilo* class, our second example.

The *Ex Nihilo* Namespace Object

One of the most serious deficiencies of JavaScript is its lack of any namespace capability. It would be nice if my_code.js did not collide with your_code.js, but that requires some work on our part. The common solution is to create a namespace object and write all the code inside it.

Listing 6-1 shows a little namespace from a picture viewer being hacked up on my computer.

Listing 6-1

```
var ns_temp = {
    // change to real namespace name!

    delay: 3,
    next_func: undefined,
    order: 'outline', // outline or random
    picture: {},
        // will become the current picture
    photos: [ // 'name' or
        ['name', 'comment (description)']
        ['lt 2nd floor',
            'Second floor, Wilson home.
```

This namespace object starts with a name. (As the comment says, the author has to think of something he really wants to call this namespace.) It continues with data properties.

I write functions after the data. Listing 6-2 shows a sample.

Listing 6-2

```
iota: function (length) {
    // iota(3) is [0,1,2].
    var i = 0,
        ret = [];

    while ( i < length ) {
            ret.push(i); i += 1; }

    return ret;
}, // end: iota()
```

(If you recognize that function, you'll know the other language besides JavaScript that was a great favorite of mine.)

All my functions are assigned to properties of the namespace object. There are no vars or functions that "pollute the global variable" in this style.

My object constructors and their prototype properties come after the other functions. Within each section (data, functions, and objects), the properties are in alphabetical order. This becomes important as your code gets longer.

Assigning anonymous functions to the namespace object properties has one feature (failing?) you should bear in mind: they will not be hoisted. Hence the order: functions precede object constructors. That ensures access to the functions when your constructors and their instance methods are executed.

If you want to get fancy, you can write your namespace as a function that returns all the properties you will need. This lets you hide true private properties inside the function (closure—see Appendix F). This little hack of mine may end up as a family Christmas card, so it's not going to be that fancy.

These namespace objects should hold all your code except for the most inconsequential little hacks. Most published JavaScript is written in its own namespaces.

Now I'll show some less common thinking. JavaScript, delightfully, encourages fresh thinking.

The *Ex Nihilo* Class

Note: "Class," as used here, refers to an OOP-style software module that defines the properties of a "family" of object instances and stores the code executed as this family's instance methods.

If an *ex nihilo* object is one created "from nothing" (more exactly, created from an object literal, as opposed to a constructor), can you create an OOP class "from nothing"? The answer is simple. JavaScript supports nearly complete object programming. Of course you can create an *ex nihilo* class.

The more interesting question is: why would you want to? It turns out there is at least one very good reason to do so.

Returning *Ex Nihilo* Objects

Sometimes you want to return two (or more) values from a function. For example, the JSWindows window_size() method returns the width and height of the current viewport. (Called whenever the window is resized.) This could be done with an array or with an *ex nihilo* object.

- `return [wid, hgt];`

- `return {width: wid, height: hgt};`

There is a simple reason for preferring the *ex nihilo* object: readability. (Note: In ES6—aka the ECMAScript 2016 standard—"destructuring" will replace this technique, but ES6 is not, as yet, widely supported.) If the function's return is captured in a size array, what is the meaning of size[0]? In an object, size.width is self-explanatory.

In an OOP language, you could define a "size" class, which would enjoy the same readability advantage as the JavaScript *ex nihilo* object, but it would certainly be a nuisance. It would be well worth the trouble if it rescued you from the cryptic size[0], but you can have your cake and eat it too in JavaScript.

With the JavaScript approach, there is one issue: what happens when we alert() or console.log() the returned *ex nihilo* object? With an alert() we will be told that we have an "[object: Object]," which is probably no help at all. With console.log(), we get:

- Chrome: Width and height

- Firefox: [object Object]

- Firebug: Width and height

- IE: Version dependent

If we had a JavaScript class, we could write our own toString() method, ensuring that we get the results we want in all browsers. (My test code depends on consistent, cross-browser toString() handling.) This would be half way between the convenience of the JavaScript *ex nihilo* class and the inconvenience of the OOP class, however. (The JavaScript constructor might, or might not, be conveniently located near the location it was used to create your return values.) There is another way.

The Function as an *Ex Nihilo* Class

The function that returns the *ex nihilo* object can easily serve as an *ex nihilo* OOP class. An inner function is an ideal location for the OOP-like class instance method we need. A reference to the inner function can be handed to the returned object as a toString property.

Listing 6-3 shows a function serving as an *ex nihilo* class.

Listing 6-3

```
function window_size() {
    var wid = ..., hgt = ...; // logic here

    return {width: wid, height: hgt,
            toString: ts  };

    function ts() { return ...; }
        // wid, hgt nicely labeled

} // end: window_size()
```

(The inner function *is* hoisted.)

With that small `toString()` included in the function that creates the *ex nihilo* objects, every `console.log()` will happily report whatever values you have chosen, formatted as you want them, and they will be the same in almost every browser you may be testing.

Actually, the Chrome console will show off its smarts by using its own display, not your `toString()` method. In addition to width and height, that will tell you that your returned object has a `toString` property that is a function. You, of course, already know that. To make it behave:

```
console.log('' + size);
```

To always get that result, I sometimes use a congenial (and typing saving) function during development:

```
function log(msg) { console.log(''+msg); }
```

Of course, if you need to know the source of your console messages, this has your console only reporting the line number of the `log()` function.

Note that there could be any number of inner functions used this way as family instance methods. This technique is not limited to the `toString()` method. (I stumbled on this technique because I needed to make my testing code work independently of the browser I was running.)

Before we go on to look at alternatives to inheritance, I leave you with one more thought to ponder. That little *ex nihilo* class was not standard OOP. Nor was it prototypal. JavaScript is a fascinating language!

Summary

In this chapter we looked at the use of an *ex nihilo* object as a substitute for true namespacing (so that your code and someone else's code can peacefully coexist, even if both authors chose otherwise identical names).

Then we looked at a simple little function that returned the `toString()` of a simple little *ex nihilo* object. The object used improved the readability of a two-result function. (A common need if you have a function that returns screen size, for example.) This was easy to write, easy to use, and thought-provoking as it was neither prototypal nor class-based.

Next we'll look into some of the problems of inheritance, including the classic diamond problem, and the ways you can use JavaScript to get around them.

CHAPTER 7

■ ■ ■

Inheritance Alternatives

C++ permits "multiple inheritance." We'll cover this next. Java simplified C++ and multiple inheritance was one of the advanced features it left out. In its place, Java featured "interfaces," originally documented as a sort of poor man's substitute for multiple inheritance, but in the end they proved far more valuable. (In Chapter 5, you saw that interfaces are now commonly cited as one of the main OOP concepts. Multiple inheritance is not.) I extend interfaces to "capabilities" which borrow from and extend both Java's interfaces and JavaScript's "mixins." Capabilities also allow a convenient replacement for multiple inheritance.

Multiple Inheritance

Many times you meet objects that combine the features of simpler objects. C++ (among others) allows an extending family to have multiple base families. This is both powerful and problematic. There were good reasons for Java to exclude this feature. Figure 7-1 shows the basic idea.

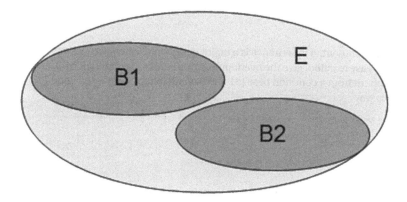

Figure 7-1.

The intent is obvious. You want a third family, E, to include the properties of two base families.

With two base families, you must decide which constructor runs first: B1 or B2. In C++ the compiler runs whichever you named first as an extended family in, for example:

```
class E: public B1, public B2 {...}
```

Of course, real base families are probably not named with convenient integers that tell you which should come first. And real base families have inconvenient issues, such as the constructors of both having circular dependencies. (A property in B1 depends on values in B2 and vice versa.) Or suppose both base families have the same name for different methods. If those problems seem simple, consider the diamond-shaped inheritance hierarchy, where B1 and B2 both extend a single family while another extends B1 and B2.

The diamond pattern is common when modeling reality. Consider B1 and B2 in Figure 7-2.

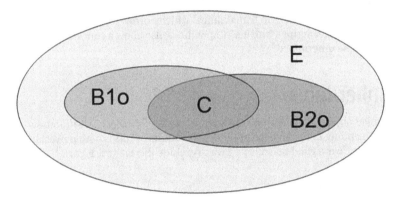

Figure 7-2.

Forget E for the moment. If inheritance is a major design tool, when two classes overlap there is an easy reaction: give the overlapping properties a class of their own, and have the others inherit from a common base (B1 and B2 both inherit from C, in Figure 7-2). You start this way:

```
B1
    C
B2
    C
```

And you modify the notation to make this a bit more compact:

```
B1, B2
    C
```

Finally, you add the class that extends B1 and B2 in the diamond pattern:

```
E
    B1, B2
        C
```

(Many C++ programmers avoid multiple inheritance entirely.)

Java simplified the class-based model by replacing multiple inheritance with interfaces.

Interfaces

An interface is the API, the outward facing properties of class software, with methods defined as "signatures" but not implemented. The class-based signature includes the method's name, return type, and the types and order of the parameters. (JavaScript methods have nothing comparable for types, both an advantage and disadvantage of having variable typing.)

A classic Java interface is Runnable, which is the interface required for an object to create a new thread. It contains exactly one method: run(). The method has no return and no parameters. The thread is created with a Runnable object. In Java you declare the interfaces that a class implements with the implements keyword:

```
class foo implements Runnable; // Java code
```

The thread knows that a Runnable object can be told object.run(). When an object is passed to the Thread constructor, the compiler checks that it has a run() method. That means that object.run() is at least guaranteed to begin execution of a method.

JavaScript has no way of enforcing such a guarantee. In practice, I have a Java-emulating thread package that has the same requirement for a run() method. Our thread-based test loads correctly but fails immediately if the run() method is missing. In theory a failure before execution begins would be even better, but in practice there is very little difference. (You can run my "thread" package at my site.)

In Java, interfaces commonly end with the "able" suffix. A Runnable object is an object that is able to "run" (by calling its run() method). A list of objects of the same type can be sorted if the family implements Comparable (by providing the comparison method the sort routine requires). Comparable objects are able to be compared.

The simplest Java interface is Serializable. It is an empty interface (nothing is required) that tells Java it is okay to write the object to disk for persistent storage. (This is a promise from the class software's author about the ability of the class software, made to the authors of other class software.)

Capabilities

In Java, when you declare that class software implements an interface, you need to write method bodies for the methods that the interface requires. In JavaScript, you can write "capabilities," which combine the defined interface (the programmer must enforce its requirements) with the data and method bodies that support the interface. Capabilities also use a little object programming to attach required methods and properties to the objects they enhance.

The term "capabilities" suggests an implemented interface providing a capability. In Java, when you implement the Runnable interface, you create an object that is capable of being run. When you implement the Comparable interface, your objects are capable of being compared (for sorting, for example). My capabilities are an object-programming enhanced way of implementing interfaces in JavaScript.

Unlike Java, our JavaScript capabilities can add properties to the objects that implement them. To avoid confusion, I permit a capability to add exactly one property, with the same name as the capability, to the object implementing the capability.

In JSWindows, a Window is a Rect that implements Closable. (To the user, it presents an "X" in the right-top corner. Clicking the "X" closes the window.) In the code the Closable capability outfits the Rect with the "X" and the attendant logic. (It closes the window when clicked. It also highlights itself—giving a red glow—when the mouse hovers over the "X".) To make a Rect Closable, the code is simply:

```
new_window.implements('Closable');
```

JSWindows was originally intended to use pure class-based inheritance. I gave up. The main object hierarchy uses class-based inheritance, but almost all the objects are outfitted with capabilities, code written using significant object programming. This lets us share capabilities among all the types of windows, for example, saving lots of programming.

If you are using JavaScript "mixins" you have seen the benefits. Our capabilities are mixins that also directly modify the objects with which they are mixed (although in a limited, controlled way).

The Window[_M[_BS]] Problem

To use class-based inheritance, I radically simplified my Window-based family hierarchy. Clearly, windows could have more features than simply being movable or button-sizable. I eliminated "closable" by making that a defining feature of windows. I finessed the title by making it the move handle. If you want a title, your window must be movable. Let's quickly design that restriction.

If we have just three features beyond closable—T (titled), M (movable), and BS (button-sizable)—we have these possible combinations:

```
Window, Window_T, Window_M, Window_BS
Window_T_M, Window_T_BS, Window_T_M_BS
Window_M_BS
```

That is eight possibilities (assuming that, for example, Window_T_M is the same as Window_M_T). What happens if you add one more capability? (You want our window borders draggable, to reshape the windows of course. Corners too.)

More generally, if you divide your object properties into groups corresponding to the way they may be used by base families, three families could have the four combining property groups shown in Figure 7-3.

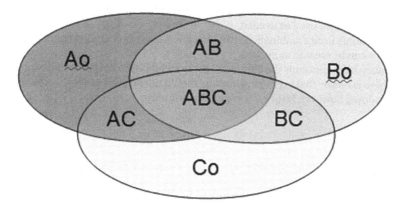

Figure 7-3.

("Ao" is a shorthand name meaning "A only.")

There are seven property groups here. Again, suppose you wanted a fourth basic class. Figure 7-4 shows some of the possibilities. (All the possibilities would require drawing in 3D, a feat that goes beyond the printed page or the flat screen. If you mentally add regions for AD, BC, and so on.)

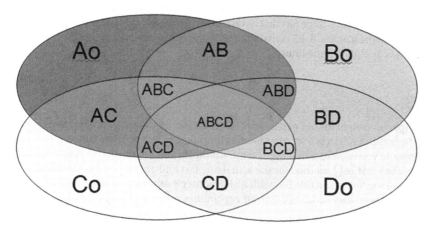

Figure 7-4.

The figure shows 13 separate regions (sets of properties). If you wanted to provide a family hierarchy that allowed any of these combinations, you would have one for each region (13), one for each combination of two regions (78 more), and so on. Clearly, an inheritance hierarchy will not solve this problem. Capabilities will.

Returning to our windows, you could have a title capability (T), a movable capability (M), and so on. In answer to our rhetorical question (what happens if you add a fourth capability?), we have a base Window to which we may add any of four capabilities. Assuming you design your capabilities so that they do not conflict with each other, you have added a capability to be used as needed.

The most commonly used combinations can be named, as before. The infrequently used combinations can be created as needed.

Our inheritance hierarchy adds the Button_sizable capability to Movable windows: Window_M_BS. There is no law that says sizing buttons should not be available for non-movable windows, however. Listing 7-1 creates this window.

Listing 7-1

```
custom_win = new Window( ... );
custom_win.implements('Button_sizable');
```

If you wanted a movable, button-sizable window, but had no inheritance hierarchy beyond the Rect, you could create one as Listing 7-2 shows.

Listing 7-2

```
win_m_bs = new Rect( ... );
win_m_bs.implements('Closable');
win_m_bs.implements('Movable');
win_m_bs.implements('Button_sizable');
```

Obviously, creating custom windows with exactly the capabilities you require is no problem. Almost as obvious is the fact that if you regularly want the movable, button-sizable window, creating the Window_M_BS constructor will simplify your work (and make it easy to add another capability in the future).

Mixins

There is ample precedent for our capabilities in the JavaScript programming pattern known as "mixins." A mixin is a set of properties that you can add to other families, as needed. Assume you want to add titles to some windows (and not to others). A title mixin might have a set_title() method for the actual title text and an add_title() method, which dropped the text into a title box with a nice border, positioned as you prefer.

You would then write code very like our capabilities code, as Listing 7-3 shows.

Listing 7-3

```
my_window.mixin(title_mixin);
my_window.set_title('Title for My Window');
```

You now have a title capability for a window that wants a title, without burdening the rest of your windows with unnecessary methods. And by adding these properties to the window, you avoid adding prototype lookups.

Calling Capability Methods

You want to be able to call your capability methods easily. Two obvious choices are to attach a property with the same name as the capability and call methods of that property, or to call methods of the underlying object. Consider the ability to draw a mask over an object (for use underneath a modal dialog, such as an `alert()`.) I named the capability `Maskable`. There are two choices shown in Listing 7-4.

Listing 7-4

```
window.mask(); // direct attach
window.unmask();

window.Maskable.mask(); // property attach
window.Maskable.unmask();
```

Capabilities as Constructor Properties

After some debate I decided against `window.mask`. It certainly looks good, but what happens as you write more capabilities? The probability of name collisions rises from highly unlikely, with a few capabilities, to nearly certain as you create a lot of capabilities. I decided that it was more robust to attach a single property to the constructor (in this case, `Maskable`) and let the capability "own" that property.

Capabilities as Single Properties

The decision to have just one property for each capability has proven itself in practice. The capability can add all the data properties and methods it wants to its own property. There is no more fear about name collisions. (Your application is about the Halloween ball? Go ahead and let your people `mask()` and `unmask()`. It will not conflict with your `Movable`'s masks.)

That decision immediately brought up another question, however. What should be the name of this property? Specifically, I thought both "maskable" and "Maskable" were strong candidates.

I eventually decided to keep the capital letter. JavaScript otherwise has no convention for initial capitals in property names, so the initial capital here (`window.Maskable`) clearly identifies a family capability. I feared that this might be confused with the initial capital for a constructor function, but that did not become a problem in practice.

As an aside, JavaScript has very few conventions. I favor adopting more. For example, JavaScript's object property names use "lowerAndUpper" capitalization: `Date.getFullYear()`. To keep my custom properties separate, I use "lower_with_underscore" names: `Pos_size.get_padding_vertical()`.

Capability Prototype Methods

One more capability choice was whether to use family-wide methods (`Maskable.mask()`) or prototype methods (`Maskable.prototype.mask()`). The former saves a prototype lookup. The latter wastes CPU cycles but lets us use our favored `object.method()` syntax.

Again, I chose the latter. Programmers are entitled to think about themselves occasionally. The name "prototype" disappears when you call a prototype method: `wind.Maskable.mask()`. The object becomes an explicit parameter when you call a family-wide method: `Maskable.mask(wind)`.

Examples

Define a `Window` as a `Rect` with a closing button. More precisely, a `Window` is a `Rect` that implements the `Closable` capability. This is the line in `Window.init()` that does the job:

```
new_window.implement('Closable');
```

Simple enough?

I expect that you might ask if we have moved the real work into the `implement()` method. Listing 7-5 shows the entire method.

Listing 7-5

```
Wobj.prototype.implement =
        function (capability_name, args) {
    var wobj = this;

    wobj[capability_name] =
        new jsw2[capability_name](wobj, args);
}
```

Our namespace object, `jsw2`, has constructors for each capability: `Closable`, `Maskable`, and so on.

We began looking at JavaScript objects with a simple example in Chapter 2:

Copy of Listing 2-4

```
my_object = {
    size: 'large',
    color: 'blue'
};
```

A common JavaScript pattern is to use this syntax to attach anonymous functions to namespace objects' properties:

Listing 7-6

```
var jsw2 = {
    Closable: function( args ){ ... },
    Maskable: function( args ){ ... },
    ...
}
```

So jsw2[capability_name] is a way of selecting the right constructor. jsw2[capability_name](args); executes the function. It is called with wobj, a reference to the window object that called its implement method, and whatever args the capability requires. (Closable doesn't require any.) This simple method handles every capability. Now let's take a detailed look at the Closable capability.

Closable

We'll start with the code. Listing 7-7 shows the Closable constructor.

Listing 7-7

```
Closable = function (window, args) {
    var new_closable = this;

    new_closable.button = new Button_close(
            window,
            window.name + '_closable_button',
        [DEFAULTS.Closable.button_left,
        DEFAULTS.Closable.button_top,
        DEFAULTS.Closable.button_width,
        DEFAULTS.Closable.button_height]
    );
} // end: Closable()
```

That's one hundred percent of the Closable code. It creates a new Button_close, correctly positioned per the specified DEFAULTS.

To be fair, the Button_close does some of the work. It knows, for example, what colors it should use normally and when the mouse hovers. It also knows how to respond to a mouse click.

The closing function was interesting. The question was, close the window (discarding it) or simply hide it (display: 'none')? I settled for looking for an on_close() function option on the window itself. The button looks for this function and executes it, if it exists. Then it discards the window, unless the on_close() returns false. In that case, the window is saying, "Okay, I've got it." and the closing button's job is done. That lets the window hide itself, if that's what it prefers.

Maskable

I simplified a bit when I said that a `Window` is a `Rect` that implements `Closable`. The `Window` also implements `Maskable` as our modal dialogs are only modal with respect to the launching window. (That let's the user look at the dialog, move the dialog out of the way to look at other windows/do other actions, and then decide how to respond. "Save? Well, let me check on these other things. I'll let you know.")

Figure 7-5 shows an alert popped up from the shield-shaped window. The default popup was neatly centered over the shield. I used the fact that it was movable before I took this screenshot. Any other windows on the screen would still be available for use. Only the shield is blocked.

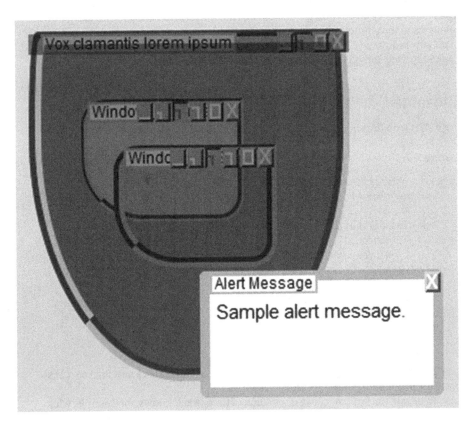

Figure 7-5.

A window launches a modal dialog by first launching a mask (translucent, it darkens the window) and then launching the dialog. The mask also grabs all mouse events and discards them, effectively turning the window "off" while the dialog is open.

The code in the window's `init()` is like the `Closable` code:

```
new_window.implement('Maskable');
```

We looked at the Wobj's implement() method in the section above. Listing 7-8 shows the Maskable constructor.

Listing 7-8

```
Maskable = function (wind) {
    var new_maskable = this;

    new_maskable.wind = wind;
} // end: Maskable()
```

That merely stores a reference to the window in the maskable property. This is used by the Maskable's prototype methods, mask() and unmask(). Listing 7-9 shows the mask() method.

Listing 7-9

```
Maskable.prototype.mask = function () {
    var maskable = this,
        wind = maskable.wind;

    maskable.modal_mask =
            new Rect( wind,
            wind.name + 'modal_mask',
            [0,0, '1 C','1 C'], 0,
            {backgroundColor:
            DEFAULTS.Maskable.mask_color} );
    maskable.modal_mask.fit_inside(wind);
    maskable.modal_mask.draw();

    maskable.modal_mask_top =
            new Rect( wind,
            wind.name + 'modal_mask_top',
            ['0',DEFAULTS.Window.title_top,
             '1',DEFAULTS.Button.height],
             0,
            {backgroundColor:
            DEFAULTS.Maskable.mask_color} );

} // end: Maskable.mask()
```

This creates two masks. The first is the main mask. It covers the content area of the window very nicely. The fit_inside() method is the same as used by the maximize() method. It picks border radii that will correctly fit the inside of the curves of the containing window. The second is an extra mask for the top line of the window. The draggable title and the clickable window sizing and closing buttons may still be available (by default, they are drawn two pixels below the top of the border). We need to make them inaccessible until the modal dialog is closed.

The unmask() method, shown in Listing 7-10, performs the opposite function.

75

Listing 7-10

```
Maskable.prototype.unmask = function () {
    var maskable = this,
        wind = maskable.wind;

    maskable.modal_mask.del();
    maskable.modal_mask_top.del();
    // wind.draw();

} // end: Maskable.unmask()
```

This capability also has a toString() method. Carefully fitting the main mask inside the curves of interestingly shaped windows took a bit of work.

Button_sizable

There are, by default, five sizing buttons—min, 0, 1, 2, and max—which you can see to the left of the closing button in Figure 7-6.

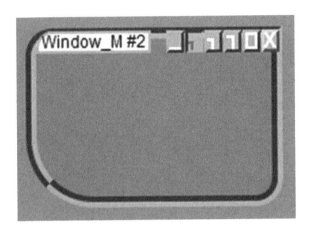

Figure 7-6.

The capability accepts a list, if you don't want all five. For example, ['min', '1', 'max'] would give you a standard min, restore, and max set. Our shield used this set, as Figure 7-7 shows.

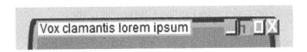

Figure 7-7.

In code, three-button sizing could be done this way:

```
new_window.implement( 'Button_sizable',
        ['min', '1', 'max'] );
```

The internals of the Button_sizable capability may not concern you. Given the simple call, above, you get the buttons you want, correctly placed (assuming right-top placement suits your needs). Alternatively, you may rewrite some or all of the 300 lines of code that this capability requires. Here we'll discuss some highlights.

The Button_sizable Constructor

The constructor has a main body and inner functions in a support role. We'll discuss the inner functions first.

The choose_default_button() function is used when you have specified more than one of '0', '1', and '2' size buttons. If you choose all three, '1' (medium) is the default. If you choose two, and '0' (small) is one of the choices and '0' is the default. The default is assigned the size you initially specify for the window.

Two other inner functions—size_larger() and size_smaller()—are used for the non-default sizes, if any. The larger choice increases both dimensions 1.4 times, which will approximately double the area of the window. The smaller choice shrinks both dimensions to 0.7 times the original size, approximately reducing the area by one half.

Now, back to the main part of the constructor. After some details, it begins by creating a "panel" (borderless rectangle) that will hold the buttons. Then it loops through your button choices, adding the buttons you've chosen onto the panel. It does some non-trivial fussing with positions and sizes to make sure that they align neatly. It also gives them appropriate names that will be used later when they are clicked. (Remember, it is the DOM element that is clicked. We have to find our way from this element to our button object.)

The last function of the constructor is to add properties to the button objects that specify the window's position and size after the button is clicked. These will be available to the button's click handler functions.

The Click Functions

There are three click functions. One for the minimize button, one for the maximize button, and one for the other three buttons (viewed from here on as ways of choosing the specific size assigned in the constructor).

The click_max_func() comes first (in alphabetical order). It creates a set of vars that it will use:

- delem is the DOM element (that reports the click)

- button is the button object that wraps the DOM element

- panel is the panel that holds the buttons

- window is the window object

- container is the window into which you will maximize

There is a major bit of architecture nearly hidden here. We deal with our own screen objects. Each of our objects (a Wobj or a family extending Wobj, and they all extend Wobj) contains a delem, the DOM element. A click, for example, reports the DOM element that was clicked. How do we find our Wobj?

The design constraint is that modifying host objects (objects provided by the host environment, and that definitely means DOM elements) is a bad practice. You shouldn't just stick your own properties on to host objects. (Upon the next revision of the browser, you could be unhappily surprised to find that the browser now uses that property for its own purposes.) There is, however, one exception: properties that the host environment expects you to modify. (You may attach a string to the title property, for example. That's what it's there for.)

The design is simple. Each of the objects is created with a name. We'll use this name in two places. In the DOM element, it is the ID of the element, a property the host provides for your own use. When the element is clicked, the element is this in its click handler. So this.id is the value of the name property we have given our own object. The second place we'll use these names is in the wobj_list, a system-wide list of our window objects. The properties in this list use these names as their property names, and the property value is a reference to our window objects. So wobj_list[delem.id] is our object. JavaScript's objects can provide simple solutions to some complex problems.

Choosable Buttons

The click functions all choose() the last button clicked. This is based on the Choices utility family. This family groups a list of like objects, one of which is chosen. This is common for radio-type buttons, for the selected window within an enclosing window, and for a menu choice, to suggest some examples. When you choose() one of the list, another must be shown in its non-chosen state. This is written in classic Java interface style. The objects in the list must all be Choosable. A Choosable object is one that implements the choose() method. To choose(), or choose(true) requires the object to show itself in a selected state. To choose(false) requires the object to show itself in a non-chosen state. Our buttons reverse their borders, from outset to inset, and change paint colors from white (enabled) to gray when you choose() them.

The Choices object's prototype methods are written in a JavaScript style, as an *ex nihilo* object. Listing 7-11 shows a sample.

Listing 7-11

```
Choices.prototype = {
        /** */
    add: function (item_to_add) {
        var choices = this;

        choices.array.push(item_to_add);
    },
        /** */
    add_and_choose: function (item_to_add) {
        var choices = this;
```

```
        choices.add(item_to_add);
        choices.choose_last();
    },
        /** */
    choose: function (choice) {
        var choices = this;

        choices.index = choices.find(choice);
        choice.choose();
    },
```

This prototype object goes on for 90 lines. Most of the functions are as simple as the ones shown here. I like the style as it is very readable, even for JavaScript newcomers who may be new to JavaScript's flexible coding options.

The Choosable interface is not expressed in code, unlike a Java interface. It is up to the programmer to add objects that implement Choosable (have a choose() method) to a list of choices. (I wouldn't object to additional compiler support.)

The Button_sizable.Button Family

```
Button_sizable.Button
    Button
        Rect
            Wobj
```

The Button_sizable capability contains two families of its own. The Button_sizable.Button extends Button (Button extends Rect, Rect extends Wobj). Again, our architecture uses excessive inheritance as this is a demonstration project, proving that class-based inheritance style design can be implemented in JavaScript. I would normally use shallower object hierarchies. For example, the Button could just extend Wobj directly.

These buttons can be punch()ed or unpunch()ed. Listing 7-12 shows that this is a simple process.

Listing 7-12

```
Button_sizable.Button.prototype.punch =
        function () {
    var button = this;

    button.borders.style = 'inset';
    button.draw();
    button.label_func('gray');
    button.disable();

}
```

The button's label_func() draws the lines that show the graphics on the buttons. The disable() method turns off the click listener.

With punch() and unpunch() methods, the Choosable interface is very easy to implement, as Listing 7-13 shows.

Listing 7-13

```
Button_sizable.Button.prototype.choose = function (chosen) {
    var button = this;

    // punch if 'chosen' is true or undefined
    if (chosen === false){ button.unpunch(); }
    else { button.punch(); }
}
```

Programmers not familiar with JavaScript will find this conditional strange:

```
if (chosen === false) ...
```

Commonly, you would test (!chosen). That would be true, unfortunately, if chosen were undefined. Hence the comment in the code.

The Button_sizable.panel Family

The panel that holds these buttons is a member of a separate family. Its code is responsible for positioning its buttons aligned nicely with the closing button. The buttons are loaded into a Choices object named buttons. This makes tasks such as setting the buttons' states very simple, as shown in Listing 7-14.

Listing 7-14

```
Button_sizable.Panel.prototype.choose = function (button) {
    var panel = this; // the size buttons panel

    panel.buttons.unchoose();
    panel.buttons.choose(button);

}
```

The Click and Draw Functions

The Button_sizable capability includes click and draw functions, also written as *ex nihilo* objects. Listing 7-15 shows the click functions.

Listing 7-15

```
Button_sizable.click_funcs = {
    min: Button_sizable.click_min_func,
    0:   Button_sizable.click_resize_func,
    1:   Button_sizable.click_resize_func,
    2:   Button_sizable.click_resize_func,
    max: Button_sizable.click_max_func
}
```

Listing 7-16 shows two of the five draw functions. The others are similar, except for the drawing details. These objects keep the buttons very well organized, which will be appreciated by the person who needs to add button choices.

Listing 7-16

```
Button_sizable.draw_funcs = {
    min: function (color) {
            var button = this;
            if (color === undefined) {
                    color = 'white'; }
            remove_kids(button.delem);
            draw_rect( button.delem,
                    0,10, 9,2, color );
        },
    0: function (color) {
            var button = this;
            if (color === undefined) {
                    color = 'white'; }
            remove_kids(button.delem);
            draw_rect( button.delem, 0,6,
                    4,2, color );
            draw_rect( button.delem, 2,8,
                    2,4, color );
        },
    ...
```

Summary

Inheritance is a principle OOP technique but is not without issues. C++ pioneered the discovery of issues in multiple inheritance (one class extending two or more base classes). The issues became extreme in the diamond pattern where two or more base classes are themselves extenders of another base.

It is common to model situations in which objects extend one or more of a menu of possible variations. We suggest a type of JavaScript mixin that we call a capability.

A capability is something that object instances can do. Unlike methods of a family, multiple families may have instances that are able to do the capability. The capability is attached to instances as they are created.

Capabilities may be the distinguishing feature separating an extending family from a base family. In JSWindows, the `Window` is a `Rect` that implements the `Closable` and `Maskable` capabilities. Because they are independent of any family, however, capabilities may still serve other families. (A `Text` family, wrapping the HTML `<textarea>` element, might also implement `Maskable` if it had a need for modal dialogs.)

By creating a distinct functional unit, capabilities help achieve the essential goal of all object programming: to separate parts of longer program units into the shortest possible programs.

Next, we conclude with some summary thoughts on designing for JavaScript objects.

CHAPTER 8

■ ■ ■

Designing for JavaScript

We chose the JSWindows project because it was well-suited to class-based inheritance. Consider the inheritance chain for the window-closing button.

```
Button_close
    Button
        Rect
            Wobj
```

Clearly, the window-closing button is a specialized instance of the generic Button. Equally clearly, the Button is a specialized Rect and the Rect is one of the objects you need to show on the screen, a specialized window object. At least this part of JSWindows fits very well into a class-based OOP inheritance hierarchy. (Not by accident. That's why we chose the project.)

But the question remains, given the material we've covered, do you have a general design approach and how would that approach effect a fresh design for JSWindows? We offer some thoughts, especially for those who come from an OOP background.

Use *Ex Nihilo* Constantly

Creation of objects "out of nothing" is highly recommended. It is a great programming convenience and can lead to very readable code.

Array Literals

We use array literals in JSWindows in creating Wobjs. Consider Listings 8-1 and 8-2.

Listing 8-1

```
wind = new Window(...
        new Pos_size(100,200, 400,300),...);
// or
wind = new Window(...[100,200, 400,300],...);
```

Listing 8-2

```
... new Window(...
    new Borders(8, 'ridge', 'orange'),...);
// or
... new Window(...[8,'ridge', 'orange'),...);
```

These pairs give the same result. A little extra code in the composition objects' constructors, to let them handle an array argument, makes our lives much easier. (Consider how often you will create an object that you need to display on the screen, in any non-trivial application.)

Styles Objects

We started using a "styles" object as soon as we started creating DOM objects in JavaScript. Listing 8-3 shows a sample styles object.

Listing 8-3

```
var styles = {
    backgroundColor: '#f0f0ff',
    fontSize: '10pt',
    textAlign: 'center'
};
```

When we create a Wobj (or any object that inherits from Wobj) we permit a styles object for those few hundred CSS styles that may be applied. (Yes, there are hundreds.) We've been using this technique for years because it works.

Other Objects

By "other," we specifically mean those properties of Wobj and Wobj-based objects that attach directly to the DOM object, not to the DOM element's style object. Will this Rect be the "name" input field? {innerHTML: 'input field here'} does nicely early in the project.

In idle moments, we ask ourselves why *ex nihilo* objects, objects that have no prototype, were first created in languages that used prototypal inheritance. There must be a moral in that story. They are invaluable in class-based inheritance, too.

Use Composition Liberally

Our second principal is to completely agree with the Gang of Four and use composition where it fits. We began the JSWindows system by writing the first versions of the Pos_size and Borders methods. Wobj was not written until these were well tested.

You looked at the Borders methods in Chapter 2. Here we'll take another look at composition courtesy of the Pos_size family.

Original Pos_size

Pos_size is the "position and size" family. To put an object on the screen you must tell it where it go and how big you want it to be. An early version allowed two optional arguments for right and bottom positions, when we chose to position that way. More on those in a moment.

Somehow the rich supply of CSS-length suffixes never found its way into our code. We've grown fond of *px* (and have been badly burned trying to work in *em* and other units). Sometimes we missed % but our styles objects let us have its functionality when needed.

In addition to letting us specify position and size, the Pos_size methods let us specify them our way. Specifically, we seldom found the CSS definitions for size (size of the content area, inside padding, and border) to be helpful in screen layout. (Apparently, we were not alone. This is now part of CSS: {box-sizing: border-box;}.)We wanted size to mean the size within and including the borders. Our pos_size objects were never measured any other way. We buried the computations needed to comply with CSS dictates inside the Pos_size and Borders methods, where we could forget about them.

Mature Pos_size

We were tired of fighting with CSS, trying to position sizing buttons left of the closing button in the top-right corner of a window, when we bit the bullet and wrote our Pos_size specification parser, shown in Listing 8-4. It proves that a little bit of regex can go a long way.

Listing 8-4

```
Pos_size.parse_ps = function (spec) {

/* BOS, opt whitespace
( digits opt(.opt digits) ) | (.digits) )
    opt whitespace
    opt ((+|-)digits)
    opt whitespace
    opt (B|b|C|c)
    opt chars, EOS */

var re = /^\s*((\d+(\.\d*)?)|(\.\d+))\s*((\+|\-)\d+)?\s*(B|b|C|c)?.*$/;

    spec.replace(',', '.').match(re);
    return {
            ratio: +RegExp.$1,
            offset: +RegExp.$5,
            type:
        (RegExp.$7 === 'C') ||
        (RegExp.$7 === 'c') ? 'C' : 'B'
    };

} // end: Pos_size.parse_ps()
```

85

The regex is, as always, powerful and unreadable. We try to compensate by having more comment (highlighted) than code when we use regex.

The regex parses position and size specs of the form:

```
'ratio [+|-offset] [B|C]'
```

where ratio is a number between 0.0 and 1.0, inclusive, offset is a number of pixels, and B (default) or C means relative to border or content area.

The ratio is the amount of the free space that should be placed on the left (or top) of the element. Free space is the number of pixels between the element's border and the edge of the container's border (B) or content area (C). 0.0 positions the element at the left (or top); 1.0 positions the element at the right (or bottom). The offset is added to (or subtracted from) this position. Once we created the ratio specification, we had no more need for the CSS right and bottom specifications. The close button we prefer is two pixels in from the right, two down from the top: '1.0 -2', '0.0 +2'. This is, by default, in the window's border. (The regex allows 1 in lieu of 1.0, if you dislike typing.)

Having fought a losing battle with CSS's minimal ability to center an element horizontally, and its total inability to center vertically, we are delighted to be able to achieve either by simply specifying a ratio of '0.5'. To center an element, horizontally and vertically, with just '0.5', '0.5' is a joy.

Composition and capabilities are similar in that they are shared across families. In JSWindows every Wobj-based element has a Pos_size and a Borders. Like objects, they help to reduce a large program into small program pieces. For example, the parser in Listing 8-4 is not simple, but it does not interact with other pieces. Its isolation makes it possible to debug, or, if necessary, replace.

Use Capabilities Liberally

Capabilities have proven their value in JavaScript mixins and Java interfaces. The latter originally found their purpose as a way of avoiding multiple inheritance's issues. Like interfaces, capabilities let us escape from complexities such as diamond inheritance hierarchies. Interfaces later became preferred for many reasons, most of which reflect their good fit with many real world objects. Capabilities, which are implemented interfaces (supercharged with some OP), share these benefits.

Some humans are computer programmers. Some humans pilot small planes. Some play tennis. Each of these is a capability that does not depend on the other capabilities. Each capability can be learned (programmed) independently, isolating a piece of the system. Tennis playing does not interact with computer programming. A human could do one or the other, both, or neither.

Our JSWindows inheritance chains could be eliminated by more aggressive use of capabilities. For example, we could add a capability list parameter to the Rect constructor. A Rect that implements Closable replaces our Window. A Rect that implements Closable and Movable replaces our Window_M. A Rect that implements Closable and Button_sizable does not even exist in our inheritance hierarchy, although it may be exactly what is wanted in some situations.

Just as programming objects helps reduce large systems to a set of smaller, independent subsystems, separating capabilities from objects further reduces program size.

Use Inheritance Conservatively

Inheritance is useful only when the extending family is a superset of the extended family. Let's return to our first figure, Figure 3-1.

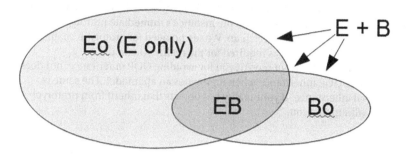

Copy of Figure 3-1

Inheritance is a valid model for E and B only when Bo is empty. This is a very specific, limited situation.

That does not mean, however, that it occurs infrequently. The success of C++, Java, and the rest of the OOP family shows this. It is also possible, as JSWindows shows, to design this relationship (empty Bo) into a system deliberately. While we don't recommend forcing systems into an OOP inheritance pattern, we do recommend using OOP inheritance when that matches the reality a system models.

When we redesign JSWindows, we will not remove the Window just because it is a Rect with capabilities. A "window" is a well known user interface component, in systems we all use. As a convenience, we will adopt the name as a shorthand for a Rect fitted out with common window capabilities. We'll make ours Closable, Movable, Button_sizable, and Maskable. This will make it very easy to create the most common windows. Our main hierarchy will be simplified to:

```
Window
    Wobj
```

We might cut out the Rect middle man, but closing and sizing buttons really need an inheritance chain like this:

```
Button_close, Button_sizable
    Button
        Wobj
```

One final note on inheritance. JavaScript inheritance chains, when inheritance is used, should be short. Possibly. This advice is almost universal. If inheritance chains are shortened when you use construction and capabilities and avoid forcing reality to fit inheritance, then we agree. On the other hand, if you are using short chains because JavaScript's prototypal inheritance grows less efficient with each added prototype lookup, we disagree. As JSWindows shows, OOP inheritance chains in JavaScript are simple to create and maintain without using chained prototypal lookups. We only use the prototype to store instance methods and never look past the instance's immediate prototype, regardless of the length of the inheritance chain. We see no need for prototype chains. Inheritance chains should be as long as required for the reality you model.

Model reality. JavaScript does not reward you for avoiding OOP inheritance, nor does it penalize you for using OOP inheritance when it provides an apt model. The same is also true of prototypal inheritance. If your reality has objects that inherit from prototype objects, JavaScript will support you.

Summary

OOP inheritance is a technique for creating two families, one extending another. The extending family is a superset of the base family. Prototypal inheritance is a technique for creating a second object based on a prototype object.

Using either type of inheritance, objects commonly have different data properties but share methods with their sibling objects. Using OOP languages, the methods are written in the OOP class. Using JavaScript, the methods may be written in the object prototype.

Using prototypal lookup chains is not efficient in JavaScript. The technique shown in our JSWindows demonstration system shows long inheritance chains programmed without prototypal lookup chains. When your software models a system that includes an inheritance chain, long or short, using JavaScript's mixed class-based/prototypal object model lets your code map easily to your reality.

Finally, unlike static OOP languages, JavaScript lets the programmer manipulate objects during execution. Objects may be created *ex nihilo*, from nothing, and object properties may be added and deleted as the program warrants. In JavaScript, the programmer can work with object properties, including their names and values. In OOP, the programmer works only with property values during execution time, a serious limitation.

We also suggest programming with "capabilities," mixins that implement Java interfaces, as one way of taking advantage of JavaScript's object programming to extend the gains made by using software objects.

CHAPTER 9

■ ■ ■

On Constructors

Some say you should never use the new operator in your JavaScript. I use it when I want to create a family of objects all varying in their data properties' values. That is just what OOP languages do. We think the huge success of C++, Java, and other OOP languages tells you that this paradigm commonly matches at least some of the realities our programs model.

Unfortunately, the new operator's implementation in JavaScript could hardly be more confusing. Knowing exactly how this operator functions may help you shine in interviews but it will not help you write code.

If you skim or entirely skip this chapter I won't be disappointed. But you'll miss this sentence:

> *JavaScript, in spite of the use of the name "prototype," is at the most fundamental level closer to class-based inheritance than to prototypal inheritance.*

You'll miss the rather complex argument behind that sentence. It's an interesting thought, but not much practical help if you just want to write code.

Constructor Magic

Let's start with the "magic" in the constructor. By "magic" I mean to criticize JavaScript, not praise it. Code that is free from magic is code that is easy to read, and therefore easy to maintain.

When I say "constructor," bear in mind that a function is not a constructor because it starts with a capital letter (although it should start with a capital letter). It is a constructor because it is used after the new operator, which is where we can start.

The new Operator

The new operator is privileged. It looks at the argument to its right (the constructor function) and dives into its internals to make certain "improvements." Here we'll look closely at these improvements.

The this Parameter

In general, you cannot explain JavaScript's uses of this with simple, regular rules. The following remarks refer specifically to this created by new.

First, the new operator creates a new, empty object that will be passed to the constructor as the this parameter. Listing 9-1 is a sample Dog constructor.

Listing 9-1

```
function Dog(name, breed) {
    this.name = name;
    this.breed = breed;
}
```

When used after the new operator, this is a reference to the initially empty object passed to the constructor.

A common JavaScript pattern that helps readability is the "Single this" pattern. It states that this should appear no more than once in any function and its single appearance should be at the top, where a new, meaningful name is assigned. Using the "single this" pattern, the above function would be written as Listing 9-2 shows.

Listing 9-2

```
function Dog(name, breed) {
    var new_dog = this;

    new_dog.name = name;
    new_dog.breed = breed;
}
```

The this parameter is also special in that you can assign properties to it, but you cannot change its value (the object that new assumes is being fitted out with properties). You cannot assign to it even if you have given it a nice, meaningful name.

The constructor.prototype

The new operator relies on the fact that the constructor function (actually, every function, because any function might be used as a constructor) has a prototype property. In our example, that is Dog.prototype. JavaScript functions are objects and you can attach properties to them, just as you can with any other objects. (Functions that are no less capable than other objects are often called "first-class" functions. These are essential for "functional programming," as in the Scheme dialect of Lisp, one of JavaScript's other forebears.)

Crockford says (*The Good Parts,* p. 47) "The new function object is given a prototype property whose value is an object containing a constructor property whose value is the new function object." Crockford's writing can be dense. Let's take this one step at a time. The result is simple.

"The new function object ..."} First, let's create a new function object (functions are a type of object).

```
function Dog(name, breed) { ... }
```

If you prefer, you could create a reference to an anonymous function:

```
var Dog = function (name, breed) { ... }
```

"... is given a prototype property..." Let's give our new function object a property named prototype:

```
Dog.prototype = ... ;
```

"... whose value is an object ..." That property named prototype is, to be precise, a reference to an object. Let's assign an object literal.

```
Dog.prototype = {...};
```

"... containing a constructor property ..." That object literal needs a property named constructor.

```
Dog.prototype = {constructor: ...};
```

"... whose value is the new function object." Well, now we've come full circle. Remember the new function object? That was Dog. So the value of our property is, to be exact, a reference to the function object:

```
Dog.prototype = {constructor: Dog};
```

When you create a function, any function (let's try another for cat lovers), JavaScript gives it a property named prototype that refers to an object. Then JavaScript gives that object a single property, named constructor, and it assigns a reference to the function as the value of that property.

```
Cat.prototype = {constructor: Cat};
```

The new operator relies on the function having a property that is an object named prototype and the fact that this object has a property named constructor whose value is a reference to the function. To give credit (or blame) where it is due, this magic is performed by the Function constructor.

The "[[prototype]]" Property

Next we come to "[[prototype]]", which you see immediately is a string in quotes, not something highlighted as actual code. This is because "[[prototype]]" is the name the JavaScript standards (ECMAScript) give to a property internal to the object being created in a constructor. (I said above that new created an empty object. Before the object was handed to the constructor, it was given this ghostly property. The value of "[[prototype]]" is a reference to the prototype property of the constructor function—in our example, a reference to Dog.prototype.)

You cannot read nor write the "[[prototype]]" nor even follow the reference. In Firefox's JavaScript, and in the latest versions of the ECMAScript standards, "[[prototype]]" is also the __proto__ property of the object instance. (You might want to forget that __proto__ exists until it is available in all major browsers.)

The Prototype's Prototype

The value assigned to "[[prototype]]" is a reference to the constructor's property named prototype. (Remember, this property—Dog.prototype, for example—is an object.) In our example, this would be:

```
Dog.prototype.constructor = Dog;
```

(Just what Crockford said.)

That assigns a reference to the constructor function to the constructor's prototype property, where it can be accessed as if it were an instance property.

```
alert(lassie.constructor); // Dog reference
```

Why? Again, that's a prototype lookup. A prototype lookup is actually a lookup in an object, a reference to which is the value of the "[[prototype]]" property. For an object created by Dog, that will be a lookup in the Dog.prototype object. Lassie has no property named "constructor" so JavaScript looks in her prototype. Lassie's constructor function is Dog, and her prototype is the object Dog.prototype. The value of that object's "constructor" property is a reference to the Dog function, from which Lassie was constructed.

"[[prototype]]" Implies

It is hard to overestimate the importance of "[[prototype]]". It refers to a property of the constructor. That implies that every object created by the constructor shares the same "[[prototype]]" property. Stop and think slowly. Every member of the Dog family, in prototypal terms, "inherits" from Dog.prototype.

Unlike true prototypal inheritance, where one object inherits from a prototype object, in JavaScript every member of the family inherits from Dog.prototype. Were we not avoiding the word "class" because of its ambiguities, we would say that the class inherits from the object prototype. This means that JavaScript, in spite of the use of the name "prototype," is at the most fundamental level closer to class-based inheritance than to prototypal inheritance.

Note that in class-based OOP, the class software creates the properties of each instance one at a time. With a JavaScript object assigned as the prototype, it is the prototype object to which the properties are assigned, one at a time, to define properties of the family. You will see numerous assignments to xxx.prototype (where xxx is a reference to a constructor) if you look at the JSWindows software.

The Dynamic Prototype

Let's take a break. How about a dynamic prototype? If you could modify the prototype object during execution, you would be, effectively, changing the class (OOP-definition: software that defines/initializes the objects in a family). In fact, this has far-reaching consequences.

It's dead simple, too. The prototype is an object and objects can be modified. Consider Listing 9-3.

Listing 9-3

```
Dog.prototype.time = "It's early.";

var lassie = new Dog('Lassie');
log( lassie.time ); // It's early.

Dog.prototype.time = "It's later.";
log( lassie.time ); // It's later.
```

This is not class-based OOP. Doesn't lassie.time look like an instance's data property? (I don't recommend writing code that wears costumes for disguises. Try rewriting so that you use time(), an instance method.)

While you consider this listing, consider the possibility (probability?) that using this technique will result in perfectly unmaintainable code. Simple? Yes. Powerful? Yes. Scary?

Break's over.

A Bit More Magic

There's a line of code implied, but not written, in your constructors.

The Constructor Returns this

The final magic is that the constructor, without a return statement, works as if it ended with a line that says:

```
return this;
```

In practice, it's likely that the new operator retains a reference to the object it creates and passes to the constructor as this. JavaScript constructors should not have explicit return statements. (Some do use explicit returns so that a single function can be used as a constructor, sometimes, and as a plain function, other times. This is a prescription for unreadable code. The built-in Date() works this way.)

With this much magic, a summary is in order.

The "Magic" Summarized

The new operator appears to be a unary operator, except that it opens the constructor function on its right and makes some invisible modifications. The first of these is to add an invisible parameter named this, a reference to the object being created.

The constructor function (call it cfunc), courtesy of the Function constructor, has a property named prototype. The value of this property is an object that has just one property named constructor. prototype.constructor holds a reference to the constructor function, cfunc. The new operator assigns a reference to the constructor's "prototype" object property as the value of a ghostly (no reading or writing allowed) property referred to as "[[prototype]]".

The value of "[[prototype]]" in the object called this in the Dog constructor is set to Dog.prototype. The value of Dog.prototype.constructor is Dog.

JavaScript, when asked for an object property that is not found in the object, will look for the property in the object's prototype. The standards call this property "[[prototype]]" but you cannot read or write it. JavaScript, when it is asked for a property of a Dog family object, will look in Dog.prototype for properties that are not part of the individual dog object.

Every object created with new Dog() has Dog.prototype as its prototype. A single object is the prototype for the entire family (class) of Dogs. This is very like an entire family in the class-based OOP model sharing the OOP class software.

Finally, the new operator retains a reference to the object that it passed to the constructor as this, and behaves as if the constructor ended with the statement return this;, passing the this reference on to its left.

Constructors Are Not for Inheritance

At first look, the task seems simple. To create an instance of E that extends B, start the E constructor by creating an instance of B. Consider the example in Listing 9-4.

Listing 9-4

```
function E() {

    this = new B();
ABOVE IS AN ERROR!

    new_e.more_props = more_values;
    ... // other E properties here
}
```

Because of the "magic" of JavaScript constructors, they are not suitable for extending families. E cannot simply embed a call to the B constructor in its own constructor.

You might want to start as shown here, but it is specifically prohibited. You cannot assign to this in a constructor. Suppose you could write the code in Listing 9-4. What would the value of "[[prototype]]" be when you create an instance of E?

```
var an_e = new E();
```

Should the value of "[[prototype]]" be E.prototype? That is the rule. The "[[prototype]]" is the prototype property of the constructor function. But why not B.prototype? Follow the same rule for the line inside E:

```
this = new B();
```

Clearly this's "[[prototype]]" is B.prototype! JavaScript avoids this ambiguity by making assignment to this illegal in constructors.

Giving the object referenced by this a meaningful name, such as new_e, does not let you get around the rule. If you assign a reference to the this object to new_e, then write new_e = new B(); you no longer have a reference to the this object in new_e.

You recall that we moved 100% of our constructors' logic into methods we called xxx.init(); so that we could call a base family's init() method within the extending family's init() method. This avoided the "magic" of the new operator and lets you write your own code, your own way.

Summary

You've reached the end. Hope the journey was a pleasant one.

And you've found out that JavaScript is not quite as prototypal as many are saying. If you create multiple objects from a constructor, all the objects created will be cloning a single constructor property so you will have a family, all children of the same parent.

And if you followed our little example, you've found that changing the prototype, on which an entire family depends, can be done as the program runs. It's not only possible, it's simple.

I'd say more, but it's time for me to get back to writing code. I enjoy hearing from readers, by the way. Ask my website for my e-mail.

■ ■ ■

CHAPTER 10

Appendices

A Surveyed Pages, OOP Principles

1) Dynamic dispatch, encapsulation, subtype polymorphism, inheritance (delegation), and open recursion. Also classes, methods, message passing, and abstraction. `https://en.wikipedia.org/wiki/Object-oriented_programming`

2) Abstraction, specialization, encapsulation, inheritance, and polymorphism. `http://www.jamesbooth.com/OOPBasics.htm`

3) encapsulation, abstraction, inheritance, and polymorphism `http://codebetter.com/raymondlewallen/2005/07/19/4-major-principles-of-object-oriented-programming/`

4) Class members, inheritance, interfaces, encapsulation, and polymorphism. `http://help.adobe.com/en_US/AS2LCR/Flash_10.0/help.html?content=00000159.html`

5) Data abstraction, encapsulation, message, method, class, inheritance, late binding polymorphism, abstract classes, interface, delegation, and generic classes and interfaces. `http://catdir.loc.gov/catdir/samples/cam032/99087328.pdf`

6) Class, inheritance, interface, and packages. `http://docs.oracle.com/javase/tutorial/java/concepts/`

7) Class, encapsulation, association, aggregation and composition, abstraction and generalization, abstract class, interface, inheritance, polymorphism, overloading, and overriding. `http://www.codeproject.com/Articles/22769/Introduction-to-Object-Oriented-Programming-Concep`

8) Classes and abstraction. `http://www.csee.wvu.edu/~ammar/cpp/cpp.html`

9) Inheritance, abstraction, encapsulation, polymorphism, cohesion, and coupling. http://www.slideshare.net/ TelerikAcademy/25-object-oriented-programming-principles-c-fundamentals

10) "According to the principles of object-oriented programming, all OOP languages have three traits in common: encapsulation, polymorphism, and inheritance." http://www.slideshare.net/snykmcajob/oops-and-c-fundamentals

11) Class, abstraction, polymorphism, inheritance, encapsulation, composition, cohesion, coupling, and interface. http://javarevisited.blogspot.com/2010/10/fundamentals-of-object-oriented.html

12) Modularity, encapsulation, and reuse (composition, inheritance). http://javarevisited.blogspot.com/2010/10/fundamentals-of-object-oriented.html

13) Classes, polymorphism, and components. http://zone.ni.com/devzone/cda/ph/p/id/45

14) Properties, methods, events, subclassing (inheritance), polymorphism, and encapsulation. http://www.dfpug.com/loseblattsammlung/migration/whitepapers/FundOOP.htm

B   Selected Books

Conflict of interest: This book was sold by Amazon. Links to Amazon for books in print are, however, common today, even in libraries, as they provide considerable information, well beyond what one might find in a card catalog.

Classics: In chronological order, classic books referenced in this book are:

Mythical Man-Month, The, Brooks, 1975, on the difficulties in developing software.

C Programming Language, The, Kernighan and Ritchie, 1978 (2e, 1988), the best book ever on programming in a specific language.

Design Patterns: Elements of Reusable Object-Oriented Software, Gamma et. al. (aka Gang of Four, or GoF), 1994, on designing software.

C++

C++ Programming Language, The, Stroustrup, 1986 (4e, 2013), classic by the original author of C++.

C++ Primer Plus, Prata, 2011.

Thinking in C++, V1, Eckel, 2000 (still on your author's shelves).

Java

There are too many Java books and your author has written some of them. This is another author's list.

JavaScript

JavaScript: The Good Parts, Crockford, 2008, a must read, but not for beginners.
   Professional JavaScript for Web Developers, Zakas, 2012.
   JavaScript: The Definitive Guide, Flanagan, 2011 (6e), not recommended prior to the fifth edition.

Python

Core Python Programming, Chun, 2e 2006, still on your author's shelves.

Visual Basic

Visual Basic in Visual Studio 2015, the official Microsoft language site, linking to their books.

C   Selected Websites

Note: The shorthand names prefixing the links (**Oop-W** for Object-Oriented Programming in Wikipedia) will be used in definitions (Appendix D) and support for selected statements (Appendix E).
   Wikipedia keeps getting better. It is often the place I begin any investigation. It is not, unfortunately, strong on this book's subject. Judge for yourself.

Wikipedia on Object-Oriented Programming, Class-Based Inheritance and Prototypal Inheritance

Oop-W   Object-Oriented Programming. The first paragraph is perfect.

Prtp-W   Prototype-Based Programming. Ironically, an excellent description of class-based programming. A good summary of the argument for prototypes as opposed to classes.

Clss-W   Classes (but beware of the first sentence).

Inst-W   Instances (objects). A very good beginner's introduction, very poor Wikipedia article.

Mthd-W   Methods. Another good introduction, but "class" must be defined broadly to not exclude prototypal language methods.

Inhr-W Inheritance. Inadvertently, but correctly, defines "classical" inheritance as OOP inheritance (as opposed to prototypal inheritance). Supports the use of "super," a term to which we object.

Cmp-W Composition over inheritance. The idea is the same, but I hope *JIOP* is less confusing.

Trts-W Traits. "Traits" may be close to, or the same as, our "capabilities," but this article is not clear enough for any certainty.

The Author's Web Site on Class-Based Inheritance and JavaScript Programming

Master Classers, a comparison of OOP library APIs (plus Crockford, on prototypal, and your author on plain JavaScript).

JAVASCRIPT CLASSES, a set of pages, most predating this book, on various class/prototypal topics. Some may be quite obsolete.

Cheryl rule on JavaScript readability.

Other Web Sites on Class-Based Inheritance and Prototypal Inheritance

Object-Oriented Programming:

Oop-1 OOP and related terms from Java's source, Sun (now part of Oracle).

Oop-2 OOP defined, including a good description of classical data modeling.

Oop-3 OOP in C# and Visual Basic; the gospel according to Microsoft (not different from classical OOP as described in *JIOP*). Cites "full support" for "encapsulation," "inheritance," and "polymorphism."

Oop-4 OOP in Python introduced, including another explanation of objects as reducers of complexity.

Oop-5 The view from Berkeley.edu, 1998. A little perspective is a good thing.

Prototype-Based Programming

Prtp-1 Overview from princeton.edu. Substantial agreement with Wikipedia. (Now, 11 Nov., 2015, 'is a' reference to the WP article.)

Prtp-2 Academic research from Université de Montpellier (France) including basic charts, a must for anyone who cares about the genesis of object programming (or who enjoys French English: "Distinction between variables et[stet] methods").

Prtp-3 Prototypes in Python? Yes, in Python.

Prtp-4 Prototypal programming in Self, Io, and JavaScript.

Prtp-5 Advantages of prototypal programming, a forum post answered by one who knows classical and prototypal in game programming.

Classes

Clss-1   Objects and classes, per Adobe. Adobe ActionScript was a superset of JavaScript (now fading, banned by Apple).

Clss-2   What Is a Class? from Sun (now part of Oracle), the creators of Java.

Clss-3   Classes in PHP. PHP, arguably the only important language without OOP, joined the club with PHP5.

Clss-4   Classes in JavaScript, from MDN. The MDN (Mozilla Developer Network) JavaScript documentation is the best single source for the language. It says JavaScript functions can be classes.

Clss-5   Classes in OOP according to top authorities like Yourdon and Booch.

Clss-6   Classes in Cobol (yes, Cobol!) "OO COBOL implements a classical object model."

Instances

Inst-1   OOP terminology, including instance in Python but applicable to all OOP languages. Good distinction between instance and class variables.

Inst-2   objects, instance methods, and instance variables, per hws.edu (Hobard and William Smith) solid re the basics.

Inst-3   Objects Defined per marakana.com courseware. Correct, academic-flavored definition (state, behavior, and identity).

Inst-4   Classes and objects in Objective CAML for a little variety.

Methods

Mthd-1   From *Think Java*, one book on Java. There is no debate on the definition of "method"—an action that an object (or class, for class methods) can perform.

Mthd-2   Methods in Ruby.

Mthd-3   Methods in C++.

Mthd-4   Methods in Fortran with OOP added, Fortran is still important if, for example, you need weather forecasts.

Inheritance

Inhr-1   On inheritance in Python.

Inhr-2   Definition from kioskea.net neatly demonstrating why we don't use terms like "subclass" and "superclass."

Inhr-3   Inheritance in JavaScript implemented via the prototype chain, which we think is suboptimal.

Inhr-4   Using Visual Basic, from fau.edu (Florida Atlantic University. Gone as of Nov. 11, 2015).

Inhr-5 Traditional discussion from oregonstate.edu including classic "is a" and "has a" distinction.

Inhr-6 Inheritance in Perl, from gantep.edu (University of Gaziantep, Turkey) stands up for Perl (not our favorite language, but now OOP enabled).

Composition

Cmp-1 Composition Versus Inheritance casts another vote for the Gang of Four, in depth.

Cmp-2 Composition vs. Inheritance, per JavaWorld (limits inheritance to true "is a" relationships).

Cmp-3 Composition vs. Inheritance vs. Aggregation (a distinction that we don't find helpful, but…).

Cmp-4 Composition vs. Inheritance vs. Association from umsl.edu, (University of Missouri, St. Louis in case you wanted to go beyond aggregation. Gone as of Nov. 11, 2015.)

D   Defined Terms

Often the most controversial portion of an analysis is the definitions. We have attempted to use terms that have (more or less) common definitions and avoid terms that are ambiguous (e.g., polymorphism). Wikipedia is particularly valuable in having a community editing process that often achieves consensus on definitions. We also check other sources, however. Our defined terms and their references include:

> **Object-oriented programming:** Oop-W, Oop-1-5
>
> **Prototype-based programming:** Prtp-W, Prtp-1-5
>
> **Classes:** Clss-W, Clss-1-6
>
> **Instances (objects):** Inst-W, Inst-1-4
>
> **Methods:** Mthd-W, Mthd-1-4
>
> **Inheritance:** Inhr-W, Inhr-1-6
>
> **Composition:** Cmp-W, Cmp-1-4

(A second dash, as in Oop-1-5, denotes the full range: Oop-1, Oop-2, …, Oop-5.)

E   Support for Selected Statements

Stroustrup, on classes and "His OOP language ran at the speed of C programs…" : http://www.stroustrup.com/hopl2.pdf. (Benchmarking C++ vs. C once showed a 3% advantage for C. He called this "unacceptable.")

"Today even 50-year old languages (Basic, Cobol, and Fortran) have adopted objects." Oop-3, Inhr-4, Clss-6, Mthd-4

"Other languages, such as Java (1995) adopted the C++ object model." Clss-1-6, particularly Clss-2

"By contrast, the "prototypal" object paradigm does not use classes. The programmer creates a prototype object and other objects are then copied from the prototype." Prtp1-4

"An object is a collection of properties (often a set, but "set" has a mathematical meaning we do not want here). Properties are named values." Inst-1-4

"Objects also are permitted direct access to a collection of functions (commonly called "instance methods") that are part of the class (in class-based languages) or the prototype (in JavaScript)." Inst-3, Mthd-1-4, Prtp-1, Prtp-2, Prtp-4

> "In OOP, a class is the software that creates and supports a set of objects, including the constructor and methods that instances of the class can perform. A class may also have methods and data of its own ("class statics" in Java)." Clss-1-6

"In class-based OOP, when Bo is empty we say that E 'extends' B, or E 'inherits from' B." Inhr-1-5.

[In prototypal inheritance] "Objects inherit directly from each other. The base object is called the 'prototype' of the inheriting object." Prtp-1-4

"If an object includes another type of object as a property, it is using composition." Inhr-1-2, but see Inhr-3 and Inhr-4 for qualifiers

"[JavaScript] also lets you create an object *ex nihilo* (from nothing)." Prtp-2

"We are not endorsing inheritance-based architecture;" Inhr-1

"We extend interfaces to 'capabilities,' which borrow from and extend both Java's interfaces and JavaScript's "mixins." Trts-W

F   Simple Closure

JavaScript, with its first-class functions, makes creating a closure a simple matter. At a minimum, you need:

- A function (the closure)

- A private declared in the closure

- An inner function (manipulator) to change the private

- A way to view the private from outside the closure

The closure is a type of constructor. It can return an object containing the manipulator and the viewer.

Listing F-1 shows a closure.

Listing F-1

```
function make_closure() {
    var _private = 0;
    return {add:add, check:get_private};

    function add(amount) {_private += amount;}
    function get_private() { return _private; }
}
```

Listing F-2 shows a main program demonstrating the closure.

Listing F-2

```
var close = make_closure(); // _private === 0

close.add(2);
log( close.check() ); // 2

close.add(3);
log( close.check() ); // 5
```

The secret here is the "execution context" of all functions. The vars and functions declared inside the function are recorded in the function's execution context. Functions declared within a function have access to that context. That lets them access vars in the execution context. (Recursive function calls would not work without the execution context.)

I use closures, primarily for animation. (They don't have viewer functions; they move DOM elements on the screen. The private values are vars like top and left. When the element moves around the screen, you know top and left are changing.) But in general, closures are too much akin to magic for me to be enthusiastic about any general uses.

G   Sealing and Freezing Objects

The fifth standard for JavaScript (ECMAScript 2015, aka ES5) provided fine control over objects for those who prefer a more traditional OOP style programming ability. To emulate C++ or Java objects, you can seal an object, as Listing G-1 shows.

Listing G-1

```
o = {};
o.bar = 1;
console.log(o); // {bar: 1}

Object.seal(o);
o.foo = 0; // You can't do this.
delete o.bar; // Nor this.
```

```
o.bar = 2;
console.log(o); // {bar: 2}
console.log( Object.isSealed(o) ); // true
```

You can neither add nor delete properties of a sealed object. You cannot change properties' configurations. If properties were writable, they remain writable. You can change their values. A sealed object is a traditional OOP-style object.

You can create an immutable object by freezing.

```
Object.freeze(object_to_freeze);
```

This is like sealing except that it sets each properties' writable value (see Appendix H) to false. You can test for this status with Object.isFrozen(object_to_test).

H   Configuring Properties

ES5 gave us configurable object properties.

All object properties have a configuration object. By default you get:

- configurable: true

- enumerable: true

- writable: true

- value: undefined

Configurable properties can be reconfigured by changing the configuration object. Enumerable properties appear in for/in loops (and in Object.keys()). You can change the value of writable properties.

You can set and reset these values with the Object.defineProperty() method. However, if you use this method to create a property (define one that doesn't exist), each of the Booleans (configurable, enumerable, and writable) defaults to false. Listing H-1 sets two properties this way.

Listing H-1

```
o = {};

Object.defineProperty( o, 'foo',
      {value: 1,
        enumerable: true} ); // read-only!

Object.defineProperty( o, 'bar',
      {value: 2,
        writable: true,
        configurable: true} );
```

Note that foo cannot be changed because it is neither configurable nor writable. A subsequent call to Object.defineProperty() can reconfigure bar.

```
Object.defineProperty(o,'bar',
        {enumerable: true});
```

(Remember that JavaScript, by design, is distributed as source code. Setting configuration properties will not slow down a malicious programmer.)

The configuration object also supports get and set properties to which you may assign custom getter and setter methods.

I   Dynamic Properties and Me

Modern languages may feature full object programming's ability to add and delete properties during execution. Ruby calls this "metaprogramming." Python calls them "dynamic properties." I first met them in Python.

On first reading about dynamic properties, I said to myself, "This isn't an object model. It's chaos." (Too many years writing Java and C++ before Java, I'm afraid. Sometimes it's good to remember how wrong you can be.)

When I started to get a little Python skill, I decided to write a Python tokenizer. (I'd written tokenizers before. My Java tokenizer had come in handy for numerous tools I had built for myself.)

Each time I'd written a tokenizer I'd run into the same issue: some tokens are relatively rare but have special needs. For example, floating point literals need a double_value property to store the value of the number, in addition to the properties common to all tokens (such as text to store the source text). Other tokens don't require a double value.

What to do? Add a double_value property to your Token object (and waste its space in every other kind of token)? Create an extending class that adds the double property (and begin complicating your tokenizer with an inheritance hierarchy)?

For Java, I'd added the extending class. I was never sure, afterward, that it had been worth the trouble. (When I first learned programming, RAM was measured in kilobytes, not gigabytes. Old habits die hard.)

For Python? No problem. When your tokenizer realized it was looking at a floating point value (it finds the period character in a number token), you just add a double_value property to the Token object you're building and move on. It was then that I began to think like a Python programmer. (Or a JavaScripter.)

Object family members don't all have to be identical. Differences are okay. Diversity is a good thing.

Index

Get the eBook for only $5!

Why limit yourself?

Now you can take the weightless companion with you wherever you go and access your content on your PC, phone, tablet, or reader.

Since you've purchased this print book, we're happy to offer you the eBook in all 3 formats for just $5.

Convenient and fully searchable, the PDF version enables you to easily find and copy code—or perform examples by quickly toggling between instructions and applications. The MOBI format is ideal for your Kindle, while the ePUB can be utilized on a variety of mobile devices.

To learn more, go to www.apress.com/companion or contact support@apress.com.

Printed in the United States
By Bookmasters